MASQUERADE

Also by Carolyne Wright

Books of Poetry

Stealing the Children
Premonitions of an Uneasy Guest
Seasons of Mangoes and Brainfire
A Change of Maps
Mania Klepto: the Book of Eulene
This Dream the World: New & Selected Poems

Chapbooks

Returning What We Owed
From a White Woman's Journal
Brief Irreveries
Carolyne Wright: Greatest Hits 1975-2001

Translation

In Order to Talk with the Dead: Selected Poems of Jorge Teillier
(from the Spanish)
The Game in Reverse: Poems by Taslima Nasrin (from the
Bengali)
*Another Spring, Darkness: Selected Poems of Anuradha
Mahapatra* (from the Bengali)
Majestic Nights: Love Poems of Bengali Women
Trazas de mapa, trazas de sangre / Map Traces, Blood Traces
(poems of Eugenia Toledo, translated by Carolyne Wright)

Nonfiction

A Choice of Fidelities: Lectures and Readings from a Writer's Life

Anthology

Raising Lilly Ledbetter: Women Poets Occupy the Workspace
(co-edited with M.L. Lyons & Eugenia Toledo)

MASQUERADE

A MEMOIR
IN POETRY

CAROLYNE
WRIGHT

LOST HORSE PRESS
Sandpoint, Idaho

Author Photo: E. Rucker.
Book Design: Christine Lysnewycz Holbert.

FIRST EDITION

This and other fine LOST HORSE PRESS titles may be viewed on our website at
www.losthorsepress.org.

LIBRARY OF CONGRESS CATALOGING-IN-PUBLICATION DATA
Cataloging-in-Publication Data may be obtained from the Library of Congress.
ISBN 978-1-7364323-3-4

Table of Contents

I Cape Indigo

II Fire Seasons

III Crescent City

IV Notes From the Stop-Gap Motor Inn

V Big Uneasy

VI Reflections in Blue

In memory of Lee Meitzen Grue (1934-2021),
doyenne of the New Orleans Poetry Forum
and Patron Saint of Lesseps Street

For Jim, always, no Masquerade

CAPE INDIGO

At First Sight

WHAM.
                    Kismet's
metabolic blow-dart
rams into my breast bone
skewers through rib cage
and cartilage, lung-sac and heart
muscle, and lodges with a *boi*
oi-oi-oi-oi-n-n-n-g-g-g

stunned shudder.

                    What
the hell? Fire power's
poker-stab. . . .
                    Cupid's curse
or Caliban's *cri - de - cœur?*

Round: At First Sight

Through the window's louvered blinds, you
glide in profile across the room, angled
pitch of your hips almost a dancer's
backlit by a single kitchen bulb.
That's all. Through twilight's translucent blinds

you glide through backlight that falls
four-square on the outside veranda where
I hover, waiting for my door to open,
glancing through the next-door window
where you glide in profile, the room

falling in four-square light onto
the veranda at my feet, next to
the studios' caretaker turning the key
in my door, angle of your dancer's silhouette
flooding my breastbone with sudden fear.

Or is it the single kitchen bulb
that silhouettes you in profile
in your studio, a reversed mirror
image of my own next door
where the caretaker turns the key

so that I can step inside my mirror
image in reverse? Next-door studio
where I will live a year beside you.
Fear's light falls on all fours at my feet,
your profile in silhouette, the blinds

half-open. Have you noticed my
moment's gaze that goes on a year
until I step into my studio
and close the door, your image
profiling mine through louvered blinds?

"Blame It on My Youth,"

I hum at the arts center's opening fête,
a tune I've heard for the first time
            on public radio's after-hours jazz

        out of Boston. I'm happy by myself
this evening, sipping a gin & tonic
            without the gin, newly arrived

        as everyone, early October's red-letter
maple leaves scraping like *papier maché* scraps
            against the windows.

    Where are you
as I chat with sculptors and novelists,
            painters and poets, all of us reading

        each other's name tags? Ah yes—
that center of stillness near a bookcase,
            you sit on a braided throw rug

        on the gallery floor, in faded blue jeans
and pressed denim shirt, one arm folding
            your crossed knees to your chest. Even then

        you lean into the next moment,
gazing into your wine glass with a sly
            smile, lip-synching whose words

        to yourself. Have I forgotten that first sight's
blow-dart has already struck?
            If anyone asked then, the question

would puzzle me. *Safe?*
Of course I'm safe: you glance up
         as I pass, your attention ripples, then

    veers away. I'm just another
woman in the room without a name yet
         as conversation swirls and Elvis

    Costello groans on the stereo, *The angels*
wanna wear my red shoes. We haven't
        yet been introduced.

    What if the cloud
of circumstance had hovered a moment
        then eased off, if the future weren't already

    stitched to the past? This evening
we are all just starting out, all of us
        too young for blame.

Watched by Whales

Sun floods the dunes this morning
    with Cape Cod's Indian yellow
        gouache, and I try to scat-whistle Herbie
    Hancock's *Dolphin Dance* between
my teeth as I bound up the swaying,

walk-the-plank steps and give my syncopated
    tap-tap-tapping on your door. "Want to come
        be watched by whales?" I ask the wooden panel
    swinging inward and the rectangle of shadow
from which you emerge, heavy-lidded,

averting your glance as the dunes' lemon
    reflections strike the planes of your face
        and I repeat my invitation, squint-grinning
    to deflect the threat. Above us,
wavering V's of geese yelp in unison

like a big band's reed section. You gaze
    down at me as if I were the busybody
        from Porlock nosing in on your private Xanadu.
    "*Say what?*" you mutter, your voice
dusty with reluctance. Have you been at work,

asleep? Is a woman with you?
    Your arm across the door-space blocks my view
        inside. I shiver in late October's sudden
    chill. *Keep it light,* I chide myself
as I stutter to explain: the season's

last whale watch, some painters, a novelist
       and I are getting tickets, would you
             like to join? I finish with some quip
       that Ahab never had it so easy, you know,
with Moby Dick, then flush as the look

on your face makes me follow the thread
       of that comment to its race-baited source.
             "No, no," you murmur, "thanks," then
       shut the door. The whole exchange: two
minutes. To your five words I've spilled

five score, shivering in the quickened
       breeze, still talking as your door closes.
             How foolish do I feel? I shrug,
       I don't believe in *All or Nothing*
at All. I've done what I could to be

a pal, drawing the line at friendship.
       I clatter down the rocking steps–
             still in my right mind, not yet anybody's
       consolation prize. From inside
your shuttered studio, you never see

the pod of fin whales frolicking
       off the prow, breaching and spouting
             in the slate-gray scud, as the captain cuts
       the engines and in the sudden lull
a young whale breaks from the ponderous roil

to leap straight up, nose to house-high tail
　　　flukes against the sky. He arcs over
　　　　　　the deck, hanging a moment like a dancer
　　　in sheer wind as the railing's length
of watchers gasps and he slides back

like a pewter blade, shelving into
　　　the wave-storm. I grip the rail
　　　　　　in a speechless breeze. I never
　　　tell you—no man has ever thrust
his summer into me like that.

The Putting-Off Dance

Humming a blues riff from far inland,
you lay the moon shells I give you
on your table's little dune of letters
that have piled up for days, unopened
as the bodies of sand dollars.
You are the man
with whom I share a wall.

All morning in adjacent studios, we move
between kitchen and work table, each footstep
tracking its next-door shadow.
November's ten-knot gale
rattles the veranda, the sidelong windows
empty of sky. In the diorama I imagine

this row of studios opens to its cutaway
dilemmas. In jest you press a stethoscope
to my wall, X-ray vision switched on full
like figments of wishful thinking.
Moon shells pile up, signs of the zodiac
look both ways. Who says *No*
is out of the question? As long as I type

your voice is the sea in my ear.
When I pause, a chair scrapes
on your side of the wallboards,
you cat-walk down the veranda
to my door. It's too late to outwit
the moment, to redouble my keystrokes

in an arbitrary gabble to reverse your steps,
erase your profile through my Venetian
blinds. Your honey and mulled wine
win this round, your tongue-tied plea
I never quite believe, but my alibis
ride a tilting raft. You give me a turquoise
amulet with broken clasp, its damage

unexplained as women who ring for you
on the downstairs phone. I set an African
violet on the sill, its petals meant to deflect
you. *Who leads?* I ask the season's waltz card.
Who follows? Our moves tell the future
in mirrors. You stumble whenever the phone

switches long-distance partners. Your zodiac
unknown: what sign would claim us
from dream's shifting dune-house?
We go back to our desks as if
to lovers, the phone downstairs
ringing its two-tone note: *Decide.*
Decide. Voices fly out of the letter piles

clamoring for answers, my blood's
divided longings. When bedroom lights go out
in this coastal town, our footsteps
echo across the floorboards,
so much diverted sleep between us.
Stalling for time, I name old lovers—

those who quoted from *The Complete Guide
to Rejection*. Rain squalls off and on
all evening like a difficult conversation.
Doesn't night's unbroken sky
arch like a serious question, our ends and beginnings
threaded on the same strand, each constellation
lined up along its own ecliptic? I fear

          your universe with its own rules. Traceries
          of North Atlantic sand between my quilted
          comforter and pillows, I scribble
          predictions in the dark while the town
          sleeps, inventing one last reason
          it wouldn't work, my body up against
          that wall, braced for giving in.

Aubade: Still Life

A length of *sari* voile draped over the curtain rod
filtering the North Atlantic's morning light.
Arabesques, paisleys of rainbow splayed
over last night's wine glasses.
One goblet tipped over on the table,
a tongue's lick of claret trembling
in its concave bell. Fingers of sun
across the room as I step, still

sheathed in dream, onto naked floorboards.
In the bed, the man sleeps. One hand
has thrown the old quilt off, his body
lean, mahogany among tangled blankets
where a single uncurtained slat of light
presses against him, his sex at rest,
legs akimbo, his arms outstretched, embracing
my shadow imprint in the sheets.

How could the two of us have slept so
in that narrow bed?
I wash in a pool of hyacinthine light
that spills from the bathroom mirror,
touching myself as gently as he did
last night, when he stepped between me
and my door. When he stopped taking
No for an answer, and my own acquiescence

surprised us both. His hands across my body
through what was left of night, almost
proved my fears wrong. His flesh entered mine
for the first time: colors penetrated,
passed through our hands like kaleidoscopic

fragments, arabesques of shadow
kneeling to each other. Now, taut
mask of his face relaxed in a dreamer's

slight smile, skin under the moustache
and beard-wisp smooth as a boy's. Now,
Ravel's *Alborada del Gracioso* plays
on the tape deck in the young painter's
studio next door. We could hear her
weeping through the wall last night
as we made love, our mattress
practicing its own blue music.

"Hello, World"

We rise together naked
    and stand before the morning's

half-drawn blinds. Oceanic light
    surrenders itself at our feet.

Afternoons we walk along the one street
    spining this narrow town, with paper sacks

of scallops and okra, or packages to mail, our laundry
    things already married in the basket.

Other days we stroll salt-crystal paths
    through pine shadow, the outer dunes

beyond those boughs shifting
    like mid-ocean swells. We riff lines

into gull-crazy air, calls and responses
    daring their way forward: one rope

looped to another, late sun in our eyes
    a lingering brilliance. Brainstorms

I scrawl onto old envelopes—
    who can tell which lines are yours,

which mine? As the tide's twilight
    fulcrum shifts, the full moon rises

in perfect opposition to the sun
    and *syzygy* is your word: love

uncoupled from need. We believe
in such pronouncements, walking home

past the shrimp boats' silvered rigging.
Evenings I chop peppers and leeks

and you stir *filé* into the gumbo,
calling me once by another lover's name.

In my bliss of unlistening, it would take
years to catch up to the heart's

subtractive powers, forgiving
both of us our losses.

Compared to What

"What's it like, you know, with him?"

the blonde sculptress from Saratoga
asks me, over a glass of *fumé blanc*
at the Ship's Table. What can I say?

On the jukebox, Les McCann snaps
his fingers, Eddie Harris saxophones a street-
wise syncopation: *Tryin' to make it real*

compared to what? His jazz-funk fusion
buzzes through my brain. Her blue eyes
unblinking through cigarette haze. What world

have I stumbled into? Which one of us
is tonic, which one flatted fifth?
Who's called you an oracle and given me

a remaindered copy of *Advertisements
for Myself*? A paperback I've watched you
bend in your big hand till the spine

broke, as you went on about the global scope
of Mailer's nerve. *Tryin' to make it real,*
I hum, snatching the bar tab

from the waiter. Lattice-work
of fish nets on the ceiling, I sip wine
that can't buy my conversation,

watch my own anger flare and flicker
at invisible cues like a school of cod
flash-turning through kelp-tangle.

As *Swiss Movement* socks it to me
from the sound system and the crowds
at Montreux leap to their feet and cheer,

I veer around the woman's question.

for Les McCann

"You know what the others will think,"

I tell you, after the first night
you tongue my breasts and part
my thighs with your circumstantial
hands. The others: painters and poets,
all brilliant women who elbow me aside
in the hardware aisles or glare past me
on the check-out lines. At gallery openings
they offer themselves to you
with their eyes, or sashay past,
spilling plates of *hors d'oeuvres* at your feet,
brushing their hips against yours.
Oh, sorry! they exclaim, and pout-
smile. Their nipples point
through stretch halter tops in Cape Cod's
February chill, Arctic-blue *décolletage.* You

glance away, shift your wineglass
from one hand to the other.
What world? Even in that gesture—
fever and mystique.

"Life in the fast lane,"

you joke that night, as we uncoil
ourselves, raw-silk reluctance and private
laughter where our skins cling.
We hold up our interlaced fingers
and compare them. Transparency
or palimpsest? The candle flame wages
a doubtful battle with its reflection,
moon's rim-shadow, my hand receding
like twilight's gardenia under yours.
Don't worry, you say. *I'm my own man,
I make my own choice.* Whose choice,
indeed. Fire and assent: whose
unacknowledged plea lets you lie here
beside this woman not quite myself
who has opened like a light-struck chrysalis
you've stroked from a pine bough?

"You can't join the throng till you sing your song,"

you tease me one evening as we sip wine
at the A House. The look on your face
should warn me, tip a balance
in my brain. *I've got the right
to sing the blues,* Billie wails
on the sound system. I shrug

and say nothing, to show you
I can take it, my reasons for being there
not about need. We're young that winter

and old enough: the all-night bar's
eleventh-hour dancers, toasting our luck,
high on calculated risk and the code
of dares-go-first, the slow-drag
racing of our hearts. *Why?*
I ask myself, and then

Why not? The woman at the bar
whose flame-colored hair snarls
into coral snakes when she notices us—

she blames me for your silhouette
pressed against mine in the strobe-lit
haze of the dance floor. What
is she thinking as she pushes aside
café tables and strides toward us,
glittering before you in a sequined

chemise that ripples over her breasts
like a waterfall? Her drink fizzes
in its stemmed glass, she lights a cigarette,

smirks at you, blows smoke
in my direction, and stubs it out.
Electric strippers shimmy on
a theatre marquee in my brain.
I ask myself: What have I stolen
from bebop's lesser gods?

"I fell in love with you the first time I looked into
  Them There Eyes,"

I hum, spooning raisins and shredded
    coconut into chipped porcelain bowls
        from Goodwill, slicing onions and green chilis
for Indian curry I've promised you, laughing and wiping
    Them There Eyes as they water,
        red in the morning as a storm foretold.

Your eyes, when you stop by for coffee,
    brighten at the preparations, then
        glance away. You hold out an invitation card
with scalloped edges the color of sailors' warning.
    Medusa's perfume exhales from the paper: a party
        to fête the fellowship she's won.

"Are you going?" I ask. "Of course—everyone's invited!"
    you protest, then stop as I tell you
        I have no invitation. *"Whose side are you on?"*
I snap, your silence so eloquent I ought
    to hear the answer, while your eyes
        could tell me anything.

They sparkle, they bubble, they're gonna
    get you in a whole lot of trouble,
        the song in my brain teases. Do I ask you
not to go? I recall the Jim Crow anecdotes you've told me
    from your younger years: *"Oh! Are you here,*
        too?" You mocked a blue-eyed socialite's

shrill of surprise as your second lieutenant's uniform
    eased over to her clique-knot, like a baritone
        shadow at the officers' club. "Are you here—
Too?" You pressed a squeal from that final syllable
    with bitter glee. Do I hear the same old song
        transposed now to a different key

between us?

Don't explain

why you've stumbled back
alone from that party at 4 a.m.
and turned in at your own door.

Don't tell me I must have
slept, my face pressed to the wall
like Thisbe, Pyramus's fool.

Your footsteps trampled gravity
on the other side. Do I forget
whose world it is? You've

earned the right to go anywhere.
What about me? I ask next day,
stepping across bare floorboards

of your studio. *Shhh,*
you hiss. *The whole world
don't need to know our bidness.*

What then? I make no edgy comeback.
I don't tell you how, under her party's
blazing windows, I wrote a card

that started, *May your prize make you
as happy as it's made me.*
Then propped a champagne bottle

in a gift bag inside her screen door.
Through her gauzy curtains
all the yellow warning signals

flashed *Beware,* and I walked home
through empty streets, wondering
what it is about you.

After the *hush now* and the *don't
explain,* what it is
about me.

Gumbo Nights

"Move away from that table,"
you tease as I help myself to a plateful

of your Creole etouffée, *"you going to end up
wide as you are tall."* All those evenings

you chuckle at your own jokes as the gumbo
shimmers with scallops and okra, shallots and *filé,*

while I stir batter for the cornbread and splash
a shot glass of burgundy into the squash chowder's

slow ochre bubbles. *"Trouble's brewing,"*
you smile, smoothing your hands over the bottle

of budget chardonnay as if it were a woman.
"Inside that thin woman there's

a fat woman fighting to get out." Out
pops the cork with a satisfying *thwock,*

to which I laugh my answer, popping
my own cheek with a finger as you light

the Gallo-jug candle with its fringed skirt
of wax drippings, centerpiece of my thrift-shop

tablecloth. The kitchen walls lean in
to listen, and I listen as Sarah Vaughan croons

Lover Man on my small radio, almost a lullaby
that winter when jazz is as new to me as Cape Cod's

lilac dawns. Dawn is a voice still trembling
in my throat, but Nina Simone's bent blue-

violet notes soothe my body into believing
in itself. Do I believe what you call

the body's shy audacity as we sip from after-
dinner jelly glasses, last of the chardonnay

smoky and pale, while you gaze at me, appraise
me, and I gaze back, matching the gleam

in my eye to yours?
                    Your knock on my door

on New Year's, weeks before, as I unpacked
the gift-wrapped packets from a visit home—

the same day one of your old lovers headed home
after a week-long rendezvous. Through my wall

two sets of footsteps hollow on floorboards
of your studio, echo-receding down the wood-

plank steps, thudfalls on winter's frost-heavy path
to the bus stop. *Stop it,* I almost told myself

but didn't, because Billie Holiday growled *"How
could you?"* to some double-dealing lover from her tiny

big-band stand inside my radio. The radio's lingering swing
as I heard your steps retrace themselves, erase

themselves from the walkway and wood-plank
stairs, canceling out all short-term memories.

"Forget that foolish week," you murmured—
your face, as I let you into my studio,

haggard with bravado. Did we know the midnight hour
had already tolled for us from the church steeple's

pale melon clock face? *Let's face the music
and dance,* cried the music in my head,

ahead of yours for a change. *A change going come,
I know,* cried Sam Cooke, a change the woman

whose fury sent him out beyond the sky
never could have known. What did we know then,

as you stood up and came around my table
to take me again as your lover? *Lover man, oh*

where can you be? sobbed the jazz women
on the radio as the woman I was then

gave in and let you come, though I was already
moving away from the table.

On Not Going in to Rags & Roses

"Stop for coffee?" I ask, this February afternoon
as we stroll from the post office
and I slow in front of Rags & Roses,
our favorite eatery. *My treat,* I add

because I sense your hesitation.
                                        You scowl
and mutter, *"Why you need coffee
this time of day?"*
                          Stunned and tongue-tied,

what am I supposed to say? You dip your head
and glance away, sun's late blare
burnishing steeples in the west end of town
where the street's curve eludes our eyes.

Should I remind you that I make coffee
every afternoon, and invite you to *come on in
my kitchen,* where you sit at my table
with your cup out? Or should I just keep standing

there—outside Rags's heat-steamed windows
with you—and say nothing? Waves of kitchen clatter
and good jazz on the jukebox wash over us
as the door swings open with customers.

How often do we stop here? You always
order the Cape Cod Burger, and I
squid stew, its syllables in the original tongue
—*lula guisada*—clinging and delicious

as the first time we made love
months before, tonguing each other's
bodies to blood swell, salt-smoothed
efflorescence.

               The next morning

you invited me to Rags for brunch
to celebrate our clinching love's deal. Your treat.
At meal's end, face shining with triumph
and abashment, you asked to borrow

the cash, you'd pay me back when
your fellowship's next check came.
                              "Come on,"
you rumble now, full of cryptic indignation
this February afternoon. *"Let's keep moving."*

Flushed with an anger I don't want
to understand, I look east—the bay's
flat gray expanse between sand-scoured
saltbox houses. Whitecaps ride the waves

like Puritan women's kerchiefs
and strand themselves on salt flats
skirting this town where no one on the street
looks twice at our differing skins.

Why don't I speak up for myself, defend
my space next to you? We walk back in silence
to adjoining studios and close our doors
behind us. What's been eating at you

today? Did you notice, through fogged
plate glass, the lesbian couple who owns Rags
glance up from coffee mugs and ledger books
spread out on their window table

and wave *hello* to us as we turned to go?

Triolets on a Dune Shack

"... snuggled in between two small glassy dunes, facing the ocean."

—Lester Walker, *The Tiny Book of Tiny Houses*

1.

We make love only once in the dune shack.
Our reflections stroke each other in the mirrors,
The pot-bellied stove by the bunk bed glowing black.
We make love only once in the dune shack.
Atlantic winds rattle the French doors,
Sand drifts against us on the bolsters.
We make love only once in the dune shack.
Our reflections stroke each other in the mirrors.

2.

Let's say: we never made love in the dune shack—
We kissed and walked away, dunes glassy around us.
We gazed out to sea, we never looked back.
We tell ourselves: we never made love in the dune shack.
We stopped short, where the weathered driftwood found us,
And turned away in the lee of the dune grass.
We never made love, we say, in the dune shack.
We kissed and walked away, the dunes glassy around us.

Round: Midnight

These coastal nights in candle-flickering dark
I ride you easy, bare-backed and bare-breasted,
your sex straight up inside me like a second
spine. After blue goblets of merlot and apple
cordial I spill on our equivocal skin,
your indulgent laughter rumbles like Robeson's
basso as I joke and sing back-up to your vowels
of Ife and Igbo, Benin and Congo Square—
syllables that tumble us into the bedcover's dunes
shifting through candle-flicker dark. I say I
ride you easy, straight up inside me is

my second spine. *Sweet, so sweet,* you murmur
and my moves groove deep, reddening the emphasis
of winter wine spilled on our skin, midnight's
tinted goblets and Benin's call and response.
I rock on your cock-horse down to Banbury
Cross, down to the consanguine root of my childhood's
oldest rhyme, where reason's bare bones falter
and Robeson intones with us in Old Man River's
candle-hungry dark. Our shadows move, huge against
drawn blinds where midnight's coastal dunes

sift through shifting window chinks, grain
by grain, moan by moan. My second spine
deep rhythm, Benin to Banbury, we rock
like Rockin' Dopsie, my oldest cradle-song
down to your Delta roads: blue country
schooling us in sweat and contradictions
of skin pressed on skin on this peninsula

shifting in sand-smooth dark. *Sweet, so sweet*
you groan as we move deep, your hands
smoothing my breasts to pleasure and

I laugh and cry as your rumble under me
reddens its emphasis and your sperm-knot
splits, spilling into my hidden river course, dividing me
into myself, as if reason's fever-trance
broke, *so sweet,* the dune-swells hold their breath
and I withhold my pleasure till your Rockin' Dopsie
rocks on home. Then we stroke and
shudder in the blues' slowing
momentum, wrapped in each other's midnight
skin where we lean toward sleep
these candle-flickering nights in coastal dark.

II FIRE SEASONS

Fire Season

Temecula, California

The cats roll for hours in the dust.
They stalk us, fur matted,
eyes green with evasion.

    Your first letter to me
    arrives from Paradise, the home
    of an old lover. Sting of ash grit

stronger than black sage off the desert,
the Santa Ana winds driving us
like reluctant fighters into each other's thoughts.

    Trust, you write, a double line
    under the word as if you can scarcely
    believe it. *Fire's still in the air.*

Mid-afternoon: the first gray flakes
through scrub junipers, phalanxes of flame
in the ironwood. *Not everything's resolved.*

    I'm keeping my options open, fingers
    crossed. I'm tired of such confusion
    in my life, this running from myself

and all that jive. Do I believe
your letter? *Where there's smoke*
there's fire: my own thoughts

    tremble, flashes under the skin
    the answer that I never mail means
    to signify—we can't be surrogates

for anyone. Not the old lover
who gives you cash for the road, though the road
out of Paradise leads to another woman—

     into these chaparral hills where I squat naked
     on flagstones by the cabin, touching myself
     as you did, in that narrow bed all winter

on the other coast. "I'm tired of running,"
you murmur as you step through my door. Your hands
under my dress are fearless as ever.

     Blue-shadowed labyrinths of our desire
     turn once again in our favor.
     We make love, our bodies dream-slow

in the stunned air, the room deep
as a cistern. Our tongues moving
in each other's mouths, we go where

     words conceal themselves, coral adders
     curled in pine slash by the cabin door. Sulfur
     and potash homestead on our eyelids,

we ignore the chopper blades, evacuation
warnings. Outside, the winds rise,
live oaks flail their arms like men

     trying to beat out the sun,
     your hands draw their conclusions
     on my skin. Centripetal rings of fire

close on the ridge beyond Far Spring,
rescue planes circle the wrong canyons,
our different bodies not quite giving us away.

Strange how the afternoon's dry ache
makes good its claim, like deer
that linger too long in the clearing.

The loyalty I ask for slithers like flame
through your practiced hands. You enter me,
and I empty my thighs of wisdom.

White

"You need someone just like him
but white." My mother's blue eyes
through bifocals, level with mine
from her executive refuge at the kitchen table.
My first visit home that year: why have I shown her
lines that he and I scrawled across
old envelopes last winter? Reciprocal
calligraphy, *scrawl and response*, I joke.
Our brightest moments, plain as day
as night to my mother.

"He's not for you." The gavel bangs
in her syllables. I swallow my shock
beyond her knowing, nod *Yes*
meaning *No* as the opening notes
of Beethoven's Pastoral in D
from my brother's Steinway grand
float out of his practice room.

"You need someone you can live with,"
my mother says. Her verdict is weeks'-
old newspapers stacked on the chair
beside her, unfiltered Camel smoldering
in its ashtray by the table-top TV,
my father at his basement repair bench
breaking a radio into frequency
and amplitude, static's modulations.
My parents changed to strangers in
marriage's unholy alchemy.

"I can live with him," I say, not
saying I already do. Deception's
dutiful daughter, I divide my chances
by another lover's silver scarab ring
he'd let slip among last winter's dunes
as his boyhood memories exercised
their blue-tick hounds. Meanwhile, I

lingered at pre-dawn's vertiginous window
in the blue uncertain flicker
of the pilot lamp, picking wisdom's
wishbone with myself.
"He's not the person you are,"
is my mother's equivocal oracle.
Who else could be, I want to ask
to sidestep what she signifies.
Neither of us can live inside
each other's skin: his letters already

remind me. Who could glimpse
through Nostradamus's darkened glass?
The mortal outcome of the most faithful
heart-muscle, both of us unjust
and equal beneath our histories–
what carbon crystal conjure
do we need for that?

Of Omission

Lifeline season, 3 A.M., and I sit up
            in late September's blaze of maple
    while you sleep on after love

on the pallet of goosefeather and blue ticking
            I unrolled for us beyond
    the lamp's penumbra. My pelvic cradle

sways, inner lips indigo
            after your deep kiss,
    my eyes' bright glide across

what's this? Slipped from your bus ticket
            your letter to some other woman?
    Daughter

the letter's cryptic diction fumbles, *Precious,*
            honey. Her name's crisp syllables
    blotted ink pinned into

your shirt pocket—not once
            hinted, not one innuendo of her
    in our year together. My blood

stunned, as if current flared
            out of an open fuse. *Why?*
    I ask when you stir, murmuring

a name I used to think was mine.
            Dawn's sudden rain scratches
    ragged nails on the window, you close

your just-awakened face, my distress
           drowning out trains' premonitory whistles,
       semaphores at the junction flashing *Yes*

No. "You talk so much," you mutter, "that I don't
           have to say a thing."
       Your eyes veer, it would be years

before memory hears the shadow
           tremolo inside the willed certainty
       of your words. Rain's steel drum

tumbles on the eaves,
           how do we finally fall
       for sleep that dawnlight?

Then wake into mid-day
           glaze, Indian summer's
       stumble-dance all afternoon?

How do we face each other across
           the kitchen table, and later the insomniac
       laundromat whose walls blare heavy metal

above the roar of spin cycle? Your hands
           folding faded denim
       are someone else's, and I can't ask

if daughter love and father love
           deflect each other like your letters'
       cancellation marks face-down

on a mirror, or if my presence
                is a contradiction in this mix,
        outside the ambit of blood-trust.

I want to go home, but
                where is that? Our walk to the level
        crossing on the day you leave, the Erie

Lackawanna's whistle is your blues, my *cri
                de coeur.* As if the vanishing point of rails
        is some other woman's peril.

Your brothers must think I

am *Miss Anne,* Miss Short-But-Sweet
slow riff laid down in this house
where your big hand anchors
mine. Underscored beside you on your grandmama's best divan,
I shiver in late December's chill
pluvial evenfall. Just off the bus from the Big Easy, am I
the first woman of my kind—not a question
on anyone's agenda—you've brought on
home to your charmed city? Nothing bright
or brushed-off mustard pollen's yellow flare about
this one. No epidermal code-switch or confabulation,
just God's honest thing: hesitation's underblues
that almost cradle the heartsure in her
place, lover, as you utter my name before
                    the cramped parlor's gathered kin
and urge the closed rose from its petal-
knot. So who am I to question my presence
there? All those sweet years-later lost between us.

Family Matters

That afternoon you ramble through swamp shadow
with your nephews, whooping some Choctaw
call-response your boyself hollered in his day.

I sprawl by myself on your grandmother's
high iron bed, reading *Go Tell It*
On the Mountain. I'm shy as wood smoke

with your family, but as light slants
sideways through window lace
I go out and sit on the covered porch

with your younger brother, Carl, the foreman
at Carbide, still in his plant uniform,
close-cropped Afro leached prematurely

gray, his quiet wife moored beside him
in blue sailcloth. They ask you—as you mount
the porch steps, boots muddy, eyes

gleaming from the afternoon's wetland
exultations—when you'll next see
your daughter. You stop: your face

a mask of shadows, eyes hardening
in their sockets. The instant shimmers
and dissolves, you step back

muttering something, and I unfold myself
from your grandmother's lap blanket
of navy plaid. Do I know you

well enough—silences that pass
as principles, questions you want
only to sidestep? Mirroring your moves,

I mean to do the right thing
but how good is my guesswork? I follow you
inside, to wicker easy chairs next to

your third brother Del, widowed
at twenty, his half-grown boys romping
in the yard where you left them,

beside him his second wife and days-old
son on her lap, swaddled in cotton
the color of sky—child so close to day-clear

he's got no complexion yet. "His middle name
is *Roy*, after his uncle," Del says, glancing at you
who scowl and look away, face flushed

burnt sienna. *What did I say wrong*?
Del's eyes ask. Does he know how deeply
you renamed yourself, how long before I learned

even one of the names your parents—grandchildren
of slaves—had given you, pried loose
in an off-guard moment in the middle

of a story you were telling? The parlor air
thickens with dread, you go to the kitchen
with a closed face to help your grandmother

turn the Christmas ham. Del spots me alone
huddled on white wicker, and settles beside me
like one of the elected brethren.

"Sister," he smiles, "in all my thirty-seven years
I've never had life so good: first shift
holding steady at Lockheed, three strapping boys,

new wife, new son—I thank the Lord
for all these blessings." I smile, and do
the silent calculations: Del with his round

boyish face claiming himself three years
senior to the eldest: you. Is he aging
himself out of teenaged fatherhood,

the shame of self-revelation
in *Miss Anne's* gray-eyed gaze? Or are you
the one much older than you've told,

another locked gate with a Do Not Enter
sign across it? How much do hidden years,
hidden names I'm hearing for the first time

matter? How to live within silences
where a man's need for secrecy
traduces a woman's need to know?

That night, in the narrow guestroom's
narrow bed, the future holds hands
with the past, and my fear is

a tinfoil phoenix whose wings
flare across our years together—
two throwaway angels

on the season's highest branch.

III CRESCENT CITY

Faubourg-Marigny

We live on Royal, between Piety
and Desire.
The old slave quarters,
shotgun flats with barred windows,
antiqued bronze plaques
and rows of mailboxes
by the door, their decor

chic-macabre: the planter's mad widow
bursting into flame,
a houseful of servants going down
like moses in their chains.
The river at the end of the street
not Samuel Clemens' steamboat road
across the color line.

Below sea level, houses of the dead
float on their pilings. We stare
at the masts of freighters
riding at anchor above the trees.
Garçonnière—the dropped roof,
rooms just wide enough to show us
what isn't ours.

Riot lights at dusk
shine on the bellies of nighthawks
and in boarded-up houses, ghost laughter
echoes down airless halls.
Someone sings gospel in the street
after the bars close, his voice
rising above Blue Mitchell on the stereo.

The last bus rattles by.
The sign on the front reads
Desire Florida. A sneaky way
to say, "Get out of town.
We don't like your kind."
The words of the mean sheriff
in the movies, reminding us

we'll always be strangers here.
We dream of springs a hundred miles
inland. Every night, barge whistles
sound the old imperatives,
underground rivers play the lethal
blues of whirlpools. The city turns
slowly on the current as we sleep.

Vieux Carré: Before the Storm

The woman she could have been
danced naked at Sky River Rock Fest years ago. Now

she sits in her kitchen, reading
Ghosts Along the Mississippi.

Her man went North. Let the Big House
burn. Oleander and flamefall.

She runs the live oaks' gauntlet.
Dauphine Street, mule pulling a tourist buggy

drops dead in the heat. Stars collapse
in the brain. That ancient conjure.

She drifts through this city where
men lounging outside the Help Wanted windows

step aside to let her pass. Behind her gray eyes,
slave moss hangs from the family tree.

Boys smoking in doorways watch her move
under watered silk, the slow dissolve

of hemline—hurricane warnings,
danger signals up and down her spine.

She counts shots in the street at night.
In her dreams, blood dries on the drinking

fountain handles. She sweeps the doorstep
with brick dust. A fix against sweat and water—

her man leaning against Doric columns,
sipping bourbon from a Ball jar.

Was he always in love with turning away?
Men who could have been her friends

walk by, staring at the ground.
Can she guess the score they've kept,

the heart's insistent letters?
The *gris-gris* bird echoes her only song—

Let your sorrows pass into the Trouble Tree.

Masquerade

She's gone again in the Mardi Gras parade
and you're home, killing time
on the front steps, examining
the beer can in your hands.
Apotheosis of nothing.
What she throws at you this time
hardly worth the sequinned
stars in her garter:
                  "You know
how it is. Bright lights, music,
how they told us for years
we could be anything. Now
what? The one thing
we've turned out to be
hangs on day after day."

It's not easy, the way the body
ages, breaks into pinwheels
while under the grandstand,
dogs in desire's hammerlock
and wishes a dime a dozen.

Out there, it's a gala evening
of lost chances. Momus Rex
rides by on his palomino
with a million-dollar smile.
Windfall profits pile up when he tips his hat
and the crowd goes wild.

She dances away from you, face gleaming
through royal-blue plumes.
"Honey, we're known

by our disguises."
Streets where she two-timed you
cordonned off.

What did you want from her
anyway? Windchimes on the porch,
fresh figs in the morning?
Cinéma vérité with its long
leader? She's buying tickets

to cities where poets die
like lovers in the Tarot deck.
Where refugees give up waiting
for the mail, and high priests
are cutting out every reference

to blood. At night you hear her
strum her twelve-string, hum in languages
she doesn't understand. Going back
to all her dropped stitches,
she could be one of the children
poking through the drainage grate
for coins, calling up ghosts
in jump-rope rhymes she's memorized in her sleep:

"Old eucalyptus knives,
handkerchief dancers,
cane flute countries
whose copper-eyed women
wail and beat the medicine drums
in the middle of your fields."

Here she comes.

Betty Carter at the Blue Room

What a little moonlight can do,
she croons, leaning into the indigo
spotlight, her dress a shimmer
against the sequinned backdrop,
her vocalese an alto sax's reed-

flutter. She breaks into scat
syllabics, working the room as if
she can't help herself, notes soaring off
into tremolo no one can side-step.
We sit with our mixed drinks,

holding hands in a berylline penumbra.
Just below the stage where
we could live by our own rules,
your dark profile, limned
against midnight, eclipsing

my lunar skin. She glides
across velvet draperies, bends
her head back in the beaded glow,
eyes half-closed like a woman
gone into ancestral trance, feather-

notes fingered in melancholy's
slow caress: *My One and Only Love.*
This is our Blue Period.
Free passes and one drink per set,
the linen-draped table where we linger

till closing, glancing into each other's
eyes as if to surprise ourselves.

What doors does she open as she sidles
between her sidemen, reshaping love's
old standards in a slow dissolve,

subverting the after-glimmer? Everything she has
is ours, the room behind us shadowlight
and nobody's business that we're here,
no other lovers between us.
We walk home from Canal Street

to save on carfare and third-degree stares
burning through nights that almost
keep their promises. Sublunar murmurs
long past denying, refrain of our presence
coda and reprise, the city's scrim-curtain

of invisible stars. You unlock our cobalt-
shuttered door on Royal Street, memory's
oblique interstices, and we slip into
each other's arms. Let a little moonlight
have its way with us.

One Afternoon on Royal Street

You are reading *Les Nègres*. I am writing
To César. The sun gleams like a gold doubloon
Over the levee and the early winter bloom
Of camellias, the blue flame trembling

In the wall heater. Sun is blooming
With a cool flame, and you are talking
Over César and the early news. I am writing
And camellias are listening past you

To the voice of César blooming like a dark sun.
Your voice is a blue flame gleaming
On the pages of *Les Nègres*. The levees are trembling
Winter's darkest gold. Listen: I am talking to you.

after Kelly Cherry

Blue Interlude: Mardi Gras Indians

In these lunar-infused late shadows
we're not each other's unpaid dues,
gratuitous blues of blurred connections,

magnolia blossoms lolling like mules' tongues
strewn across Garden District lawns, not hued
high enough for the night's relentless weather.

Under Antares' pre-dawn flare
what theme and variations outed from Eden
do we count on? Could we brandish

compassion's magic staff like shamans
second-lining on Lundi Gras, feathered
and sequin-suited Ninth Ward krewes,

their spy-boys crying *Iko Iko* into red-lined
strife, King Zulu's regal havoc meeting
Wild Tchoupitoulas on the battleground—

coconut throw and dogbane poultices
dividing the scarlet tide of your fears
from my own? In this harsh paradise

where shadows of ancestors look the other way
past the conjure women on Rampart Street,
are we canonized by starfall, or do we plagiarize

the ancient verities to save ourselves?

The Way We Were

• • •

Four A.M., the love-sick poet in the shotgun
flat next door turns Barbra Streisand
up full blast on his stereo.
Every decibel-damned pre-dawn
for three weeks we stagger from jagged dreams

to dial in vain our latest ultimatum.
Our own phone's ringing in our ears
redoubles through the wall where
we can hear him grab the handset
like yanking calamus up by its root, and shout

Whitman to us out of the receiver—
"*Who goes there? hankering, gross, mystical, nude!*"
He stomps the floorboards with such fierce
flourish that the diamond needle leaps
and skitters across the grooves like the scrawny

tomcat that yowls feral serenades
along the back fence.
           "Stop it, Frank!" we yell
though we know he falls further for himself
the more our anger tunes him in.

From Whitman's *pent-up aching rivers*
he yawps
           and at this impossible o'clock
my dawn stupefaction sags. I try to placate his fitful
random soul. *Do I contradict myself?*
I too let Whitman have his way.
Very well then I contradict myself.

                              . . . and Barbra
goes on belting the old torch song's
score never settled, letting each of us
have it.

                    • • •

The two men in the garden flat behind us
argue about other lovers, their voices
through our bedroom wall pitched high
in the pipes' corroded copper. Is their fight
a duet or a duel? First plot twist
or last act of reciprocal scorn? Do long-term lovers
need to double-deal, or test their evasive
moves on denial's sliding scale?

Listening too hard, we embrace each other
on our side of the wall, while their stacked heels
clack in circles on the hardwood
floor, slam of their patio door
shudders through the building,
the suddenly hushed dark.

The quip I let slip to others—their *high
decibel affair*—travels fast as a game
of telephone, with a gossip's gusto
back to them. Swaying in our shared
backyard, I squint through smoked glass
one afternoon at a solar eclipse
and they burst through the gate with glares
that could have melted sunspots. Quick
and silver, their tongues scolding
a blue streak, my pyrrhic told-me-so,
they lash me off the flagstone patio.

On our side of the wall, we sway together
with Lady Day turned down to a murmur—
our lives, we joke, everybody's business
but our own. All winter, kerosene's cobalt
flame trembles in the wall grate, foghorn
blasts from freighters navigating in the channel
pilot our fears upriver through the Mississippi's
shifting shoals.

· · ·

In the warming weekends after Mardi Gras
our neighbors set tubs of mock orange
on the patio. The poet next door
hangs X-rays of his cranium
in the window. His skull glows
between security bars, a weary
sun in its corona of curls. Weekdays,
he hunkers in a wheelchair
under the crepe myrtle, and points
a derringer to his temple.
                              Two ex-girlfriends
from Delaware have moved in, one black
one white: bird-of-paradise sarongs and
bikini tops, string-section muzak
on the stereo. He calls them Slidelle
and Tripper Tina, they snap Kodaks
of his antics, the word balloon goes
"*Bang*!" over the pistol barrel and his Shocked,
Shocked look.
                    Next door, we make love
under languid blades of the ceiling fan.
Only our flat is cool and blue-shuttered.

• • •

Someone wraps the mock orange tubs
in burlap and loads them into a U-Haul.
For Dallas: That's what Frank tells us
as the van drives off down Royal and turns right
onto Desire. After his girlfriends clear out
—"my sister wives," he sighs, though there's
more LSD than LDS about him.
He shows us prints of himself
humping xerox machines, his privates
smashed against copier glass as coins
clatter in the slot and the green
copy light flashes on and on and on.

He's just been suspended from his adjunct
instructor's poor excuse for a sinecure,
and he sneaks into the office after hours,
scrawling "*Footlong Franks,
Ha Ha*," on every memo, his testicles
suspected of endless duplication.

At the department's annual fête
Frank clambers on-stage, unbuttons his shirt,
and begs the famous guest writer to scribble
a felt-tipped Aleph on his breastbone.
A guard with a nazi moustache
wrestles Frank to the floor and leads him away.
After the bail bond he never
asks for his job back.

• • •

In the antique furniture emporium
I shrug when you ask
Which chifferobe? Aren't
freshly painted bedroom walls
enough, scrape of our forks
on bone china, blue Japanese peonies
in the sofa cover? Under
polished wooden floors: brick tiles
and the waterlogged black soil
of the Delta. What about the heart's
binary code: we're happy and unhappy
in the same breath? Wine blurs
white in our throats, nothing between us
and the flood line.

Endecasyllabics: About the Women (Alma, Ruthie)

The lion-maned poet holds court on our blue
divan, reminiscing on her Aegean
days—tramping the beaches of Santorini,
bare-bouldered Hellenic hills almost too bright
to countenance—she steps into her husband's
huge sandal prints. Tawny cloud of her hair flows
down her shoulders, ashes from her Virginia
Slims scatter over the sofa's blue roses.
She props naked feet against the arm rest and
asks us: "Who else could have understood that sky,
that purest cerulean picked out by stars?
Whose words burned into the oracular stones?"
We exchange looks—are we supposed to answer?
His feet were more bruised, his form more broken than
her rose, burned to ash in Orphic shade. But she
goes on praying at the altar of his art.

· · ·

We empty her ashtray and refill her glass,
sit cross-legged on the polished wood-plank floor
eye-level with her ankles. Outside, through cracked
jalousies, Ruthie the Duck Lady roller-
blades by, in red lace-up boots and Santa Fe
flounced skirts, Jackson Brewery straw hat jammed down
over her greasy curls. A clutch of mallard
ducks, adolescents still fledged in yellow fuzz,
are waddling as fast as their flat orange feet
can slap the cobbled paving stones behind her.
Behind them, a buggy driver hauls back on
his mule, yells at Ruthie, *Hey, baby! Move on
over!* But she slow-skates straight ahead, curses
stream between her teeth in a blue billow. Her
ducks veer off, spooked by the buggy's painted wheels.

Endecasyllabics: About the Women (Ruthie)

"She's not out of touch with reality, she's just not interested."

—*David Richmond, photographer of Ruth Grace Moulon (1934 - 2001)*

I want to talk with Ruthie, discover
who is this woman, inside the Duck Lady
façade? The roller skates, thrift-shop wedding gown
and veil, the fuzzy ducklings that parade
behind her through the Quarters on Mardi Gras.
Rumors of burly, blue-uniformed police
watching over her, asleep on Jackson Square

park benches. I find her in a nameless bar
on Dauphine Street, plucking at her torn voile skirt
and runs in her pilled cotton stockings. She glares
when I ask to take her photo: "That'll be
a dollar." Her drawl is steely, her outstretched
fingers ending in carmine-painted claws. I
falter before her scowl, her desiccated

voice, her figure, perched on a broken-back chair,
tough as a folded bird. I hand over
the dollar, aim and focus—she sits up straight,
grin-grimaces for the flash. Then she nods, turns back
to her glass with its Jax Brewery logo.
My deeper questions? They never had a chance.

Endecasyllabics: About the Women (Meredith, Melody)

Half-sloshed since early afternoon, Meredith's
perched on a bar stool at Napoleon House,
whiskey glass in one hand, stabbing the air with
a freshly-lit Filter King in the other.
The life of the party! She thralls our thirty-
something crowd, banters with the men, and corrects
everything I say. Eyes stinging in blue
nicotine haze, I clench my smile, hide my hurt
deep in my sleeve, till Melody—whose sleeve is
air, her left arm stolen by childhood cancer's
rebel cells—takes me aside, says, *That woman*
envies you so much that everything you do
is wrong. Your youth, your health, your man: you have it
all. Blinded by such wealth, I can't see how soon
Death will slip his love-blade under both women's

sleek black frocks.

Blue Triolets

Bright Moments with the Blues and You

Ellis Marsalis on piano every week at Snug Harbor.
Art Blakey and The Jazz Messengers at The Village Gate.
One hot night at The Cookery: Alberta Hunter!
Ellis playing "Syndrome" at Snug Harbor.
Miles turning his back on everyone in the Arena.
Terence Blanchard's first solo at The Village Gate.
Ellis ending his set with "Zee Blues" at Snug Harbor.
Sarah Vaughan's *Só danço samba* at The Village Gate.

House of Blue Lights

We were writing a book on the blues together.
We sat at jazz club tables with the candles lit.
We studied chord changes and the devil's measure.
Such big plans! Our book on the blues together.
On Desire Street, we heard the devil's engines backfire.
Aphrodite shimmered onstage in an indigo light.
We did our best with that book on the blues together.
We stood up from that table, blew the candles out.

Blue Room

So much love and trouble in that room
When Aphrodite shimmied between tables in indigo light
And the devil's dance band struck up a bluesy tune.
So many hopes ran into trouble in that room.
Miss Mouth, you used to call me, *Lighthouse Grin.*
You weren't trying to change me, not those nights.
So much love and trouble in that room
Where Aphrodite shimmied between us in indigo light.

Another Country

*The enemy of my enemy
is my friend.*

—Bedouin proverb

Every night, counting tens and twenties
into the safe behind the Buddy
Bolden poster, I cash out. Every night
you ease in to this tourist bookshop
just before the minute hand nudges
nine. You nod, then withdraw
into your own foglight and riverdusk, so absent
among the shelves that blonde debutantes
lingering by the Fodor's Mardi Gras display
let their pocketbooks loll open
from tanned shoulders. From the counter
I watch you thumb through Rimbaud
and Aimé Césaire, Bellocq's portraits
of Storyville quadroons, evening's women
with their faces X'ed out. You glance
at me once: lovers signal each other
underground like shadows from opposing
shores. Could I understand

silences you need to survive?
I never tell you of the black man I'd seen
stopped by a white cop in Louis Armstrong Park.
The officer barked orders
into his walkie-talkie, and the man stood
flint still, legs spraddled, tin
lunch bucket and denim work shirt dropped
to the dirt beside him. He stared into nothing
above the patrol car's strobing

blue cherry. Scapegoat or suspicious
character, how could he withstand
such danger? A new anger rose
in my throat, no place
for me to say anything. Stopped
by my own skin—whatever I did
only he could be pistol-whipped
back into this scene.

In the French Quarter's afterhours air
I close the bookshop door.
You help me swing the blistered shutters
into place, drop the long-stemmed hooks
into metal eyelets. On Royal Street,
my hand stratified in yours, Napoleonic
coats of arms and the Stars
& Bars tacked across grillework
windows—the Faubourg Marigny's
categorical shorthand—your stories
ride their boxcars through pine barrens,
spar with the shadows
of slave catchers, make a clean
getaway under a tungsten moon.
You inveigh against blond
CEOs in T-shirts and cutoff jeans
like surfers at Newport Beach,

feet propped on desks of old-growth
teak, sneering at the rules
they make you live by. In that
storyboard you stand, arms limp
at your sides in a suit coat and tie

that would never change anything. *They'd
destroy me at a word*, you say. A scary
satisfaction in your accent.
You rail against the middle class
as if I weren't. Do you
forget that I'm here—
on your side, no one
you need to get even with?

I'm ashamed of memory's complaints.
You are faithful then, walking us home
down the drive-by streets, *poète maudit*
as householder, no safer than I
in anybody's crosshairs.

This Crescent City winter, I am foe
of your foe, flesh
of your flesh, questioning
easy truths I've lived by. I don't know
the score, the difficult history
of our differences. I think all losses
can be recompensed, all heartaches
we deny each other across
the years claimed for ourselves.
In that other country where anger
erases our names from each others' mouths,
our younger selves let themselves
into their indigo-hued front door

and entwine in desire's *pas de deux*
in a language that almost spells *forgive*.

The Divide: New Orleans

I step into The Olde South
Gift Shoppe, out of Chartres Street's
mid-day swelter. The doorbell's
falsetto tinkle, the glacial
wall of A/C pouring over me
like a broken levee's floodwater.
Hey honey! the lady behind the counter
chirps. *How's every little thang?*
She nods, her bouffant hair-do
blue-rinses the air. *Miss Lucille Ann
Boudreau, Proprietress*: the plaque on the wall
speaks in Garamond. *Kin I help you?*

I lean against white wicker,
gaze at the trays of pralines
and guava jam, chicory coffee and grease-
stained bags of beignets. The Mississippi's
yellow silt rises in my throat—
two months since my body
has let down its blood-cycle.
Just looking, thank you.
Strands of Komus krewe beads
looped over crinoline, antebellum
hoopskirts on armatures. Step N
Fetchit postcards. An entire shelf

of Mammy dolls. What in god's
name do I want here?
*Sit right down, honey. Heat's got you
tuckered out.* Miss Lucille chatters on,
her customers floating through the pastel air
like crepe-paper flowers. Then you

step in, the bell's jangle
burgles the air, your figure obsidian
against the mullioned window.
You smile, pull out the books
you've bought me: *Song of Solomon*
and *The Bluest Eye*.

All the doors in Miss Lucille's face
slam. *Get up out that chair,*
miss, less you mean to buy it.
Gratuitous regrets: you halt
by the masquerade ball mannequins,
your face frozen into a Benin mask,
heartwood's mahogany cheekbones scored
with the slashes for *resistance,*
fear. The only face that Miss Lucille
Ann would ever see. What is
my face saying then? *Not this?*
not you? Blood debts coming due,

we have to become our own doors.
I put your books in my straw bag
and stand up. I want to tell her,
"Miss Lucille, sometimes our shared skin
is the surface of the moon, sometimes
just another alphabet in which
*to spell **goodbye**."* I take your hand
and we step into the blistered street.

Blue Mitosis

"God bless the child that's got his own."

—Billie Holliday

Vasectomy, you say, when I tell you
two moons have left the sky
their legacy of tacit shadows
since I've missed the beat of bloodfall.
We sit in the front room's blue
backed director's chairs, our profiles
against the whitewashed walls
clean as a crime scene's outlines
on the polished wooden floor.

How so, I ask. No other sail's
hoisted in this bottlestorm.
You lean back, in your eyes
a blackbird's sidelong glimmer. Appraisal
or subterfuge, who could tell.
That angle of the shoulderblades
all wishful thinking, my speculation's
kern and ligature. Was it that April

morning in the Baton Rouge hotel,
careless with sweat and the redbird's
love notes in the oleander?
Our hands moving so smooth
over the thighs' chromatic scales
we caught all the body's nine
gates of desire unguarded.
What do you want? you ask

that night, after I've called the clinic
on St. Charles, the test result
a plus sign—antibodies clustered,
enzymes coupling on a laboratory slide.
You take me on your lap, nuzzle
my breasts already swelling.
My daughter in Phoenix, you say.
Thirteen, almost a woman. Almost

old enough to cost you everything.
What about the unbudgeted
expenses of the heart? Economies
of scale, our lives so hidden then,
terminal forgivenesses of flesh
we ask ourselves to be responsible.
That dawnlight of fog and riverdamp
you tense in the clinic's waiting room

as if the verdict were a life,
while I sit with the other women
to break the body's thrall.
Medicine's mandated circle: mandala
of circumstance, my blood pretending
we haven't yet made up our minds.
As if the verdict were the other story
we go on telling ourselves,

that inner dialogue of bile
and bloodknots, an album of secret
descendants who never had a chance.
Afterwards, we cradle cups of hot chocolate
in Burger King, plastic chair-molds
tipping us forward, ache between my thighs
a tincture of cells spreading over the rest
of our lives. Sorrow's plea

in your dark eyes, my luck
uncoupling from yours. Outside,
streetcar tracks past the clinic
still empty of rescuers. I want to ask,
Isn't marriage a mitosis in reverse?
Fused nuclei of egg and sperm, only then
can the heart begin dividing. God bless
the child that almost was our own.

IV NOTES FROM THE STOP-GAP MOTOR INN

Majesta Blue: Mothers and Daughters

I hope he marries you,
says your mother, Majesta,
as we sip Cokes
in her beige-green living room,
curtains drawn against the azure glare
of Phoenix. I shiver in the air conditioning
and murmur something. Her dark face
is kind, a map of direction lines
unfolding at a word—June's wedding specials
that shimmer on the muted TV
stealing her thoughts
this last day of our visit.

I'm fifty now, I been around,
and that boy need to settle.
What can I say? You're out shopping
with your daughter, your long-limbed
thirteen-year-old, almost as tall
as you as she pouts in the den that morning.
Your college teacher's salary
won't buy her spangled boots
and hot pants at the Vista Grande Mall.
That child so spoiled, your mother says,
I kick myself. I had my chance,
I could have raised her.

She shakes her head, curls
just beginning to silver, ring
of her second marriage gleaming
on her finger. *Girl's Momma across town*
with some no-count man, my son her Daddy
in his own world. All conversation

long, Majesta's glances signify
My son is your man now.

I sip my Coke and nod, my thoughts
hooking and unhooking themselves
from judgment. I try to breathe myself
into her place: what would I do,
all those years since she left Ponchatoula—

the first husband's purple marks along her jawline,
her children scattered between grandmothers'
clapboard houses and the mill,
slipping their own lines into the next generation.
All that she says to me—veined stones
falling into a chalk-lined well.

What does she want me to ask of you?
By the time she was my age, you,
her eldest, were almost grown, a few years
shy of your own unintended fatherhood.
I don't tell her about the clinic
in New Orleans, the child we ended
just before the moon's last waning.

You step in then, screen door
banging behind you, city transit passes
in your shirt pocket. Your daughter
is back home at her mother's—tearing
the gilt wrap from your gifts, birth-stone's
belated gleam at her throat.
Does it matter how old we are, how close
the generations, chronologies that finally
line up in Majesta's eyes?

She was fifteen when she married,
your heartbeat a drum in her belly.
Hello, Son, she murmurs as you ease in,
dipping your head with a guarded smile
at this tableau: mother and the pale woman
who could have been her daughter.

Through Bus Windows: Seattle

We make love on the floor
of your brother's unfurnished guest room,
mornings he walks his postal route.
An apartment complex five blocks
from my parents' house in View Ridge.
The neighborhood's color bar
a slow dissolve, we take this closeness
for a sign, our bodies flushed
against shag rug in the crepuscular
diffusion of half-closed shades.

Your father must never know.
My mother's whisper flares above the spin
cycle, her laundry space behind World War II
shipping crates stenciled with his name.
He bends over oscilloscopes and vacuum
tubes, safety goggles in the high-intensity
glare of his workbench. My brother
fingers Scarlatti and Couperin
in his practice room, the harpsichord's
black-key registers.

Days we prowl Coast Salish displays
at the Burke Museum: Tlingit masks
of ravens and wolves, Haida potlatch blankets.
Then perch with white wine on Jazz
Alley's spider-legged stools, waiting
for sidemen to ease in with their horns
for the sound check—through the stage door
a gritty breeze, and homeless vets
swaying to their own beats, purple
hearts like blood stains on their sleeves.

At the Obon festival, late July, we watch
Nissei women raise their chrysanthemum fans
as they circle the tiger drums, chanting
to the ancestors, a chorus of lanterns in
their moon-folds as evening deepens. But
we're cool, we don't stare at black professors
holding hands with their kimonoed wives—
couples whose steps we hope to echo.
In crowds that witness the spirit harvest
our differing skins mingle like anyone's.

At night, we ride the bus back to the same stop
like teenagers. We know you couldn't
walk me home: betrayed by the rainy
green light of my city, your shadow
never stumbles over its own doubts
at my parents' door. I phone you late,
you and your brother pouring Georgia
moonlight into the tape deck with Aretha
and Ray Charles. My brother lingers
in the hallway and rolls his eyes.

How does this old score become our song?
My father grins into whiskey
and TV. *Jungle bunny. Jigaboo,*
he mocks through Cosby. The expert's
last word on the subject. My mother folds
clothes in the kitchen and keeps her face
to herself. Why do I play along? I am
such a good girl, I want only to outlast
the dawn, keep quiet till the moon sets
in uncertainty's blue kimono sleeves.

The day we leave, we make our own ways
to the Greyhound depot. My father idles the car
in the lot, my mother walks with me
to the boarding gate. *Do you want*
to meet him? I ask.

                      No, dear,
I'd rather not: her face with its contours
of disbelief.

                 Oh, I say. *Okay.* My last words
with her before departure: *I'll call you*
from New Orleans, once we're home.
I hug her goodbye. What good to say

more, to try to change any generation
but my own? My cowardice
my strength—my eyes don't search
for you, waiting in the bus seats
you've saved us, minutes between our life
and the only family I might ever have.
From the platform my mother
looks up at us, one hand raised,
her watery brave smile like a clue
to her own diminishing.

Does she see how our faces, gazing
back at her through the bus window's
tinted glass, make their own chiaroscuro
and shadow-play? Could she sense
how the future's double blade
would cut its secret deals with us?
Late sun strikes our eyes as the bus
pulls out of the terminal,
the blood currents under our skin
in the same dark as anyone's.

On Learning That I'm Not C. D. Wright, Couple Walks Out of Maple Leaf Bar

The Dirty Dozen Brass Band is second-
     lining on the p. a. system, a direct feed
   from WWOZ's command post above Tipitina's

Uptown. At the Leaf, poets are gathering
     in a slow swirl—Jimmy and Martha and Lee,
   Bonnie and Maxine and Brother Blue

with his finger-popping soft shoe—
     around Everette at the bar, swizzle stick
   in his vermouth, in his white linen

suit jacket like a man who should have just
     dismounted from a five-gaited Walking Horse,
   a smooth ride between tobacco rows.

Pads in the shoulders to bulk him, conceal
     rib slats ridged as a zydeco rub-board,
   carcinoma sculpting its pulmonary tunnels.

And where is my man, Roy Otis?
     Fingering a page of Walcott or Soyinka
   in a corner under the Tiffany torchiere

with the librarian poets from Loyola.
     In spaghetti strap frocks and kitten heels,
   spangled *bustiers* and plumage of paradise

flounced skirts, they flutter close,
     rhinestone crucifixes winking in their cleavage.
   Roy Otis's head dips with a warm

rumble of breath into the uncatalogued
        space between them. I won't confront him
    later: who could change this need?

I linger under the Maple Leaf shingle
        for who knows what. *Feets can't fail me now*
    the Dirty Dozen chortle in a caterwaul

of cornets, tumble of tubas and the tumbler in Everette's
        trembling hand as the white-blond and bleached
    blue-eyed couple sidle over and announce

they've driven all the way from Little Rock
        since dawn to meet me. *Who?* Jarvis
    and Jolene. My would-be students from

Fayetteville. *Okay. But I'm from Seattle*
        I say. "You're not C.D.?"
    I'm not. Their call my response, fast as a

scat attack and fade. *But I'll read good as any*
        stand-in! "No deal," they wheel on stiletto
    moccasins, stepping deep into the ozone

daze of Carrollton, the Dozen played out
        in afternoon's decay. Then Roy Otis
    is behind me, Lee beaming at the crowd

from a lemon gel glow over the tiny
        stage: *You're first.* Shook leaf, I stumble
    toward the podium on fail-safe feet.

Who else knows it would be
        years before I stop taking
    No for an answer?

Celestine Dozens

Except for your adamantine battle-plan and High John's root,
No tongue-scumbled eloquence of yours
Ever would drop off the charts, you
Rascal's trafficker and right-hand man,
Gut-bucket crooner and come-on king,
Yanking your silver spoon from my back-talking mouth.

Slow-dancing in the Funky Butt on Rampart
Edging Congo Square, you run your big hands
                down my blouse, and Saint
Xavier's sisters in their Rue Toulouse convent

Cells downriver flagellate themselves into a
Lather. In the strobe lamps' flicker,
We tango, wrangle each other into sweet

Unreason, raunch, and righteous grind.
Nice work while we're getting it, low-
Down damnation blesses us with
Ecstasy's bent-blue measure, until I falter and you
Rustle some torch-singer's satin camisole to the floor.

Jam-boogying us into a wing-tissue
Web, you connive the late shifts of desire.
Bodies' bruised rhythms filter
Your tincture of unanswered longings, my
Kelvin units of regret.

Note from the Stop-Gap Motor Inn

"The man who crosses the street may be already out of reach."

—Bertolt Brecht

Blues librettist, piano vamper,
transposer of the heart's iambics
to the ideographs of anything goes,
I'm a fool to leave you.

I've traded you for this
Dead-end town, this South-
by-Midwest zipcode. *What the hell
for?* friends ask. *Don't I know*

a good thing? I tell them
I've led a charmed life.
Whatever I wanted
I got. Whatever I didn't

drove off alone. In a country
where it's dangerous to say *No*
to strangers, I've walked the streets
wearing my Silent Majority look,

my Welcome to America complexion.
I've got no talent for concealment,
and no profile but yours
is missing from the picture.

What would the true believers say
if they knew? The preacher
who crosses the street to avoid me?
Who, if I asked the time of day,

would turn his digital watch dial
off? *Too late to change us, lady.*
Too late to take the next train
or erase the lovers pressed back

to back in the Rorschach blots,
in a town where everyone thinks
memory is enough. Who's laying bets
we get out of this alive?

I'm drawing my own geography
of cowardice, and you're home, not even
whistling Dixie to remind yourself.
You know the old score—

those who live in the dreamstates
of the saved, calling themselves
the Beautiful People: your name cut off,
a broadcast across enemy lines.

Heat Wave: Liberty, Missouri

I can't wait to see
that evening sun go down.
In this first-floor hotbox,
no Billie or Bessie or Big Mama Thornton
to remind me where we've been—

New Orleans, easy city
where a white woman's dark-skinned lover
could disappear into the Creole wards
while the nay-sayers shrugged
and went on pruning the brown leaves
from their family trees. City

where we walked home from the Quarters
past the multi-colored stalls
of the fruit and flower market,
cries of the Cajun vendors.
Where we shot the bolt of our blue-
shuttered flat in the Faubourg-Marigny
and made love under the ceiling fan
as mid-summer rainstorms swept the yards
and lightning touched down around us.

Here, derailed from my big-city expectations,
I'm on my own.
Whatever I choose to make of it.
Every suitcase I unpack
a concession.

Dogs in the front yards
bark at my accent and my bedroom-
colored skin, the red dress

I wear Thursdays that says
I don't give a damn. Through jalousies
the neighborhood watches—I'm part
of all that's wrong with America.

Only the radio gives the facts.
Twenty years to the day
from Selma. Twenty years from the hoses,
dogs, the demonstrators lying in rows
in the squad cars' shadows.
Two blocks from the Kappa Alpha house
with the Confederate flag
hanging between white columns.

Every night, someone stands under my window
smoking Camels. I lower the bedframe
from its closet, sleep in a room
with screens unlocked
and a fan that drowns out
the footfalls of intruders.
Every morning, I get right up
against day's burning wall,
the *I Have a Dream* speech
fading from air above the marchers.

What else could we have said
even if I believed my life here?
If I dreamed the crossed sticks
on the lawn, waiting for evening
to burst into spontaneous flame?
One signature in the wrong place
and this old world of have-to's

got me good, twenty years
from the Freedom Riders
and Rosa Parks' *I'm tired.*

We know which side this town took.
My parents are proud
of how far from you I've come,
justifying the looped shadow
that falls down between us.
They don't see how I stand
before the bedroom mirror,
touching my nipples to the glass.

Loan Call (Almost a Ghazal)

I'm making love to him in dreams Sunday night
when the phone rings. *Honey, I'll pay for it,*

his voice reassures me, reversing the charges in my single
room. *I'm buying a house here in New Orleans!* His voice
in the receiver sweeps me up. "How will you pay for it?"

I ask. *Easy, honey,* his voice embraces me in my rented
room, Missouri's ice-rimed February night. *It's
a duplex on Piety, just 40 K, with tenants' rent it'll pay for it-*

self! But honey, his voice strokes me naked
in my visiting teacher's narrow bed. *The down
payment. I'll need your help to pay for it.*

"How much?" I ask, folding myself into his closing
costs. How much could I help him to pay for it?

Four thousand, honey, his voice rolls that shotgun
house's blueprint over me. *That's all I need to pay for it.*

Half my savings. I don't tell him it's half my savings.
"I'll need a promissory note," I say. (Is that the term?)
"I'll need your signature to say you'll pay for it,

you'll pay me back." His voice in the receiver
shifts its tactics. *No time for that.* The closing date
pours its single digits over me: how I'll pay for it.

This week, I need the check this week. His receiver voice
righteous and single-minded, he will have his way to pay for it.

Why do I let myself be buffaloed?
Why doesn't my voice stand its ground in the tinny
mouthpiece, before I rush to pay for it?

No evidence but a handwritten chit and
a xerox of the check I write to pay for it.

I never hear the other woman's movements next to him
—does she set the diamond needle down on "Nobody's Business"?—
as he tells me where to send the check to pay for it.

Is she adjusting shoulder straps of her night-dress
blue as collusion, already packing his book shelves
and calculating moving costs: how much she would pay for it?

Does she guess that it's me on the phone with him
tonight, how much each of us will pay for it?

Canzone: Head-On

The two heads turned away from the head-
on crash, turned away like dolls' heads from each other's
in the pick-up's crumpled cab, each averted head
still, gray and bloodless in the probing head-
lights, strobing beacons of patrol cars on the highway
shoulder in Ozark dark. The mountain boy's and girl's head
each turned away from the other's in the last head-
long swerve into the bus grille's blinding dark,
as we passengers clamber from the bus's shuddering dark
through the accident's sprung windows, clutching our own heads
and groaning as we jump, drop, and stumble toward lights
of the aid cars, shadows of heads in the revolving light.

Oh shit! The driver had shouted as the midnight bus met headlights
on the mountain curve out of town. He swerved to head
off the oncoming . . . *Shit!* The bus bucked once, twice, light
flooded the windshield, sleepers slammed awake against seat backs:
    dome lights
and smoke, groans and oil stench choked the aisle with another
cry: *Jesus! Help me!* A woman pinned between bulkhead lights
and the fuel line as the rest of us scrambled from windows into light
of helmeted medics' lanterns. Why did I make my way
in blur of my broken glasses toward the crumpled truck? *No way
they had a chance*: an officer pointed to the two heads, averted in light
glinting off whiskey bottles in the crushed cab's reeking dark,
each face still forming its last grimace to carry into the dark.

Why can't I look away from these faces to avert the dark?
Blind drunk, had the young man swerved toward bus headlights,
then, too late, away? Had his girl blacked out before dark
smashed through? Why was their last protective gesture, dark
as instinct, each to turn away, their unprotected heads

away—each to meet the end alone against the head-on dark?
I can't stop thinking—their bodies in the crushed cab's dark,
their bodies down there where the engine rammed in, no other
truth but crumpled blood-cages in a metallic frame, no other
truth so brutal . . . But I have to wrest myself from blood-fallen dark
toward ambulances, X-rays, glare of the ER waiting room. *This way
we survived*: my call wakes you pre-dawn, in shock's numbing sway.

At dawn, a stopgap bus—stopping in every town along back roadways
through the flat cotton plats of the Delta—reaches New Orleans by dark.
I rise from the aisle where I've held my head in my hands all the way
to meet you in the station. Is it out of your way
to meet me, take me home in a cab that stops at every light?
So many vehicles! So many streets going every which way!
We hold hands carefully as unuttered thoughts, all the way
to the shotgun bungalow I'd helped you pay down. You step ahead
and let me in to the empty front room, my undamaged head
still reeling as you show me around: the loving way
you've sanded and varnished the antique moldings. In the other
room, the loving way you pull me into bed, and I ask for another

minute to ready myself in the unpainted bathroom at the other
end of the shotgun hall—this moment to touch myself, wash away
trapped passengers' groans, patrol car strobes stroking those other
heads in the vertigo dark. This moment to towel my other
saved face dry. Under the towel, an indigo night-dress, dark
with love stains. Not my size. Dress of another
woman. I carry it out to you: "If there's another
story I should know . . ." *Oh shit,* you snap off the light
but I glimpse your dark face, gray with fear, light
drained from our making love, the unnamed other
woman's dress crumpled between us, silence averting our heads
in sleep's blinding dark. All night, my head

flood-lit with images in reeling dreams—those gray heads
drained of their breath, turned away from each other
as I turn, in fear's clairvoyance, toward you, then away.
Would we face, in dreams through that headlong dark,
how we'd avert our own lives, the rest of our light?

"I Thought You Knew"

On the patio of Café Ponchartrain,
Darla's treating me to lunch
to celebrate my almost-safe return
to the City That Care Forgot. In the toothed
shadow of potted palms, Darla's drawl

uncoils the latest gossip: Sibyl the lonely librarian
—in an outer ring of our circle of Big Easy friends—
Sibyl has just moved all her things out
of her new boyfriend's house. "He's not
her *official* boyfriend," Darla says. "She can't claim him
since his long-term lady's back in town."

I'm only half-listening, because heavy breeze
insinuates the scent of bougainvillea spilling
over Garden District walls, last week's head-on
collision in that other state still throbbing
in my brain, and Darla's going on about how Sibyl

is alone again, crying every night: "What a reward,
clearing her out after she helped him move,
months ago, into that house . . ."

                Darla pauses,
glancing at me: "that house he—Roy—bought
on Piety Street. But now *you're back in town,*
and . . ."

         And what? I start
awake, reek of oil bilge seeping from the river
at the end of the street, the levee bulging
as if to burst . . .

I finally catch on: *"So it's*
Sibyl!" I slam my hand on the table,
Darla's platter jumps and spills red beans and rice
across the flagstones.

"I thought you knew!"
Darla's gaze abashed, violet eye shadow
darkening her lids. "I thought you all—you three—
had some kind of *understanding!"*

"Give me her number," I snap, snatching the paper
out of Darla's hand and dialing the café's
ancient pay phone. Sibyl sobs nonstop
in my ear as I light into her: "How
could you? You saw me with him everywhere—
Tipitina's, Snug Harbor, the Maple Leaf!
You knew the score!"

But Sibyl's weeping
heaves from the black receiver: "He said it was
maybe over between you, not everything's
resolved, and . . ."

"And you wanted to believe him,"
I growl into black holes of the mouthpiece.
How do I bring myself to say, *"I'm going home*
now to have it out with him . . ."

I shouldn't have told her that.
But I don't mention her grubby night-dress
I'd found under a towel on the bathroom
nail. The one thing in that house
she'd forgotten—I wouldn't
be giving it back.

"Get Out of This House"

"Quit your hollering and shut the door,

the whole neighborhood listening,"
you growl when I burst in

shouting the other woman's name
and pummeling at you in the front room's
plaster-hazed air. In spite of fury's

blood-tide in my eyes, I have
this accursèd gift: I can see
myself as you do, a cartoon mouse
you hold off with one lean arm

like a cool-eyed celluloid cat.
"She called to warn me," you chuckle
without smiling. *"Said you were so mad,*
you lopsided." One big hand wipes
tiny circles on your carpenter's apron.

So much for making common cause
with women, I flash before I light
into you: *bastard, asshole,* and
that final slur I'm ashamed of,
the word I never thought
I'd utter. *"Get out of my house,"*

you snarl, your features a carved
mahogany mask. *"Not until*
you give me back my part of it,"
I say. What in the moment's tension
nails my wits to this answer?

How much was that down payment?
Such a paltry sum today—in those days

half my savings. Your righteous rage
deflates, you sit down heavily on
the arm of the blue floral sofa from Sears
you bought on sale with one of your
earliest paychecks. Your head hangs.
"What do we do now?" you look
up, asking for a decision we have
to make together. I gaze back. It is

one of our closest moments.

V BIG UNEASY

Credo in Blue: New Orleans

*"Darling, I understand
this is the Year of the Dog,
so please be careful."*

First day of the hurricane season,
lover, our year of precarious living,
so please watch your step. Don't swallow

that bayou stoopdown, or prowl like your own
best fool through Creole colonial archways
around Jackson Square. Your scared bravado's

up for grabs, don't let anyone catch you
drowning your troubles on the levee
where the self-congratulators gather like dust

off brewhouse barrels at the Jax plant
for some stud-bucket's hop-light
mimicry. Where it's all about gimmickry

of gimcrack and fanny-whack,
backslap bluster and manic calm–
dissolving metaphors of market share.

What matters here are midnight's special
effects, that everlovin' light that shines
in barrel-bottom darkness, who can shake

its bars? Someday we'll fumble with doomsday's
diamond clasp, why try to hustle it?
Even if our choices make themselves

we've aided and abetted—risk and fast action
for which the heart holds the stopwatch.
No one can usurp refulgent nights

the mockingbird warbled all moon's-arc long,
mirroring its own music in every trill,
the way we catch ourselves off-guard

in the same silhouette of listening,
a different bird in each beveled segment
of reflection. Where some other lover

stares back at us from windowpanes
slick with rain-shadow. What to do
then with the other half of our heartbeat,

late storms' vernal under-rumble,
that hell-bent rhythm's ritual rant?
What does Frankie say to Johnny

as she points the revolver
through the transom? Gratuitous blues
our back door's slant of woman-shadow.

All over the city, women whose dials
tick toward empty, women who haven't slept
in days. Nobody likes to be found out

but whose crepuscular sleight of hand
could coddle us? The bed where we enter
each other and move apart in bloodlore's

wordless flux—not some bogus rapture
or patched-up aftermath. Not some heart's
division stealing a homeless plea. Ours is the real

simulacrum, abacus of betrayers, the spleen's
beads clicking across algorithmic strings
the way unhappy lovers spread their theories

of grievance over a palimpsest of grief.

After Summer Gives Itself Away

You buy me an Afghan necklace
for my birthday, and we take photos
of each other in SoHo, leaning against ironwork
gates where motorcycles are chained
for the evening. In another city,

your other woman hangs her night dress
on the bathroom nail. She mutters
about trouble and bad luck,
and curses me. An edgy glee
to your voice, we talk around her

in third person. This afternoon, we're safe
from what's unspoken, licking Rocky Road
cones and wandering these narrow July
streets of the East Village. We gaze
at the Frog Jazz Band carved

in weightless balsa in the Afro
Imports window. My eyes
meet yours watching mine: palimpsest
inside the glass, Louisiana Delta
blues in your pupils. Evening,

we see *Gandhi* at the Ziegfeld
and leave holding hands, our shadows
fractured in the dazzle of marquis lights
like wished-for explanations,
reflections rippling across plate glass

down the avenue's escape routes.
Walking home, we talk about injustice,
world hunger, Kingsley's brilliance
recreating a whole subcontinent of strife.
In my small room, wine in chipped goblets

pulls us into each other's arms.
All night, your hands glide over me,
dark searchlights across
an ivory field, no more than skin
between us: the rose's deepening flush,

cool murmur of the after-pulse.
Lines blur, blend, interlace
what's yours, what's mine.
Hush now, you're free this time
from what I need to know, blues fade

long gone into the brain. Our blood's song
on the edge of sleep
threads a wordless path cell-
deep into an oblique dawn. How far away
you are inside me.

Epithalamion in Blue

I'm not about to hold a gun
to your head, but lover the brain
the body want to say it: believe
it's you, it's time—this time
to get it down. In the ink's
indelible vanishing acts.
The alibis that revise themselves
wherever the blue skirt lifts
and summer breaks in upon itself
catching one or the other of us
off-guard, dressed down for our own betrayals.

In the blood's panic-song
we're so often somewhere else
paying our dues long distance,
but even when the tongue sleeps
and the words fall all over themselves
we've got to play out every blue note
on the scale—bebop, Brahms or backstep,
or the *birohi*'s solo wail our mothers
told us never to settle for. No way around
the body's double-time, or else we walk
that walking bass line by ourselves,

there where the heart can talk itself
into anything, taking its dangerous chances.
Who did we think we were?
Ebony Adam and ivory Eve
undoing this nation's original sin
in our own bodies? Ideals we meant
to depend on, Effie White crying *I'm not going*
from jukeboxes in the corner bars. Now

you take my hand in the nameless colorations
of the street, my summer dress
a shimmer in the gritty breeze.

Hours later in the fifth-floor walk-up,
we make love in a tangle of borrowed sheets,
your hands with their scent of another woman
raising my nipples to hard red light.
Don't ask me to forget this.
Transgression: so sweet, that woman
you undressed in another city
as if you were hardly there, as if anyone
could have been responsible. Collective
melancholy—I touch you now
where the blessed cicatrice flowers.

In that other city where the heart
tried not to go crazy, you know how a season
can cave in, your best intentions
turn against you. You know
about sending money home to a lover
while she traded your shadow
for another man's. How did you like
those heartwounds, soldier? Don't tell me
you misconstrued those damages.
All that we've risked for each other
we hold against the shadows.

Independence evening truth serum,
a taste of your own medicine
sears our lips—lighting up our flash-
forward fallbacks. What we're here for.

Generations more than the fluvial tease,
the glisten of rivers reversing
their directions underneath our skins.
Hard lovers of a decade half-gone
we navigate these avenues for all
they're worth, as day glows into night
and we cross out the unforgiven dates.

The clock's face collapses
into its bent black hands, the alarm
needle between them snapped off.
The whole weight of the city
holds us up, and nothing can stop us
from crossing that middle-of-the-road line
but ourselves: roman candles arcing
upwards into indigo light
like a cartoon artist's dialectic,
sparking each other, sweet freedom's
bondage season just a kiss away.

"While the cat's away . . .

the mice will play . . .
in New Orleans"

That's all the note says
                    when I slide it
            from its long white envelope,

Times New Roman 12-point type
                    on plain white bond.
            No signature, return address,

or stamp, just a blue-gray postal franking
                    with a Crescent City zip.
            "Oh hell," I mutter,

forgetting myself in the college mail room
                    as Baptist secretaries gasp
            and almost drop their Bibles out of bulging

faux-leather handbags.
                    Who sent this? I demand
            of spackled white walls, bruised

linoleum floor and fly-specked fluorescent
                    tube lights overhead. Is it
            a warning or a brag?

Who sent this? I ask myself,
                    fear quickening its rhythm
            in my pulse, blues guitar solo's

low wail from the sorting room radio
                next door. *Who sent?* My voice
      a wisp in the midst of heartfall

as secretaries edge toward the corridors
                like shadows running from themselves.
      Who?—whose words blurt slowly

from blur and fury as my guesses
                falter. Sweat under my breasts
      breaks cold, and I sway

to the shakes within as the glass
                and brass wall of postal pigeonholes
      turns and curves away in my peripheral sight

like a freight train with two lights on behind.
                Who sent this? I climb aboard
      my last thought, clutching the nameless

letter, my days in this town
                sand in a shattered hourglass.
      All my mind's eye can see

is the life-sized floozie on the Bourbon Street
                swing, Barbie-doll legs in fishnet stockings
      pumping in and out of the club window

as *The Stripper's* bump and grind
                blasts from the jukebox.
      My man is prowling the Vieux Carré—

will I ever know which rival paramour
      is taunting me?

No Place Like Home: New Orleans

No room for complaints in a hard freeze.
You spend every day, this two-faced
January, under the floor struts
among shattered cinder blocks
and animal detritus, cast-iron
toy Packards dropped in a moment
of distraction by boys in short pants
from before the wars.

Miner's lamp on your forehead, bagfuls
of plastic elbows and T-sections,
a tin of galvanized joint compound
and the kid from the corner hardware store
crawling beside you with the wrench kit,
you don't need a thing from anyone.

Teaching yourself how to fix it,
unscrewing a half century of copper pipes
splintered lengthwise like bamboo,
you replace an entire understory of fixtures
on a night too cold for remorse.

Above you in the kitchen, I act out
my part of the bargain. I rinse grease
from supper plates with water hauled
in buckets from the street spigot.
Scrape at former tenants' decades
of neglect—dry rot dissolving the doors
and window sashes, mouse trash in drawers,
dead icebox and wringer washer sinking
into sagged planks of the back porch.

I who have returned from up North
where all the pipes are insulated,
carrying the one space heater from room
to room. The house you've bought
with a loan you wanted me never
to mention, with papers you never show me.
This house I never asked for.

Through knotholes in the floor
you and the boy fit pipe sections together
like Tinker Toys, sprawled shank to shank
on the littered sublevel, up to your elbows
in corrosion. At dusk you surface, cobwebs
clinging to your shirt, coveralls stained
with Delta silt. You watch me
move between table and stove
with the appraising eyes of a speculator.

That night I walk to a neighbor's house
to wash my hair. She tells how thermostats
in the projects are locked at 50°,
how the body chilled too long
loses its sense of temperature, how little
stands between us and the frost line.
Her voice quavers with the earnest tones of those
whose income is off the books,
who can do only so much to help,
who always have to be careful.

I walk home alone
down the gun-point street, your silhouette
turning away from the window.
Midnights we retreat to rooms at the far ends
of the house, I with the space heater
and you with your working man's contempt
for my helplessness.

We don't make love, we say,
because of the plumbing.
Because I too would rather move away
or get someone else to repair it. I too
among those to blame for this city
you say you have no choice but to live in.

Because windows and walls give way
no matter what, and houses built on pilings
finally submit, and no one can be prepared
for everything. Because the boy
under the floor is so much more willing,
his skin so much closer to your own.

The Gondola: New Orleans World's Fair

*"Millions face starvation from drought
and civil war in the Horn of Africa."*

—National Public Radio

I

The airborne gondola glides
on its spider's thread back and
forth across the darkened Mississippi,
a double strand strung each night
with tiny Koh-i-noor lights,

every car a Steuben pendant
swaying with its pair of lovers—
men with softening 24-carat
gleams in their eyes, women
whose eyes outshine the moon.

Flagpoles on the International Riverfront
shiver in cross-drafts from
the Algiers bank, flag cables
clanging on steel, stirring the heavy folds
of client nations' colors.

II

We sit on the glassed-in terrace
of the Riverview, lovers who wait
for news in the language of unsaying
between the atrium's champagne
fountain and the house-high palms.

We're here to make amends—
the other woman's night dress hanging
from the bathroom nail, the letter I tore
in half, the slap that skidded my glasses
across the bedroom floor.

From the TV above the bar
children's famine-shadowed eyes
follow our every gesture.
In the news anchor's litany
the have-nots' ratio, names

of grain-gruel villages he tells
like breaking strands of pearls.
The Creole waiter at our elbow
pours our drinks. In his frock coat
he could be a preacher from Soweto

standing in a chiaroscuro of lamplight.
The menu's parchment folios, weighted
as press releases: *World looks into hollowed faces*
of the Eritrean drought. Our own faces
shadowy in plate glass, fractured

in the fly-eye prisms of the table lamp.
We eat in silence, avoiding glances.
When did we stop questioning
the etiquette of those who possess,
everything we've said we're not.

III

We turn to watch the fireworks display
on the river's theme-pavilion walls.
Pyro-technicians light their nitro-
glycerin flowers, each spent flash
floats downwind in an ash-petal haze

like souls released from judgment.
The gondola stops, a string of pleasure craft
stunned by a fire fight, travelers
agreeing to any terms of surrender.
We put our stainless flatware down.

What do we have to complain of?
Are we ready to unsay the blame?
The letter retyped, the night
dress given back, the slap
dissolved from the face.

Around our table huddle children
whose skin has given up
covering them, glass barter beads
around their necks the deflated
small change of that year's revolution.

Paper-skinned infants dangle
in slings, their weight measured in milligrams.
The children wizened figures under
Red Crescent sheets by the time
TV satellites transmit their images.

The waiter in his knife-pressed vestments
picks up our crumpled bills. Outside,
the gondola lets down its lovers
gently, like crystals slipping
from the ends of a chain.

Stress / Disorder

I. 1040

I bring you a jelly glass of white wine
as you lean into the desk lamp's
saffron pool of light, reworking the last stanza

about an ambush near Phu Bai.
Mid-April and your W-2 forms
sit untouched on the kitchen sideboard

next to the cassette deck playing
Miles's *Black and Blue.*
You're paying memory's dues. Debits,

credits. Your silence an undeclared war
full of buried weapons, the gunshot
wound you never name, my fear

and fascination. No one is exempt.
I've double-checked my own columns of figures,
schedules I've finally earned enough

to admit to. I've signed and dated
my return, licked the bulky envelope,
paid my damages to Uncle Sam.

Would you walk me through these trigger-
happy streets to the Bywater Station
to make the midnight deadline?

The back of your raised hand
tells me *Yes, honey, just let me
get these lines.* I sip my wine,

watch your dark head
bent in that arc of concentration
I love: humming slightly, scatting

the new phrases as they come. Pen
stop-starting in sweet brainfired
syncopation on the page.

"What about your return," I ask
for the third time. You half-turn,
glare at me, the lamp's molten light

doing a slow glide across
your forehead: *Don't need no IRS
to know my whereabouts!*

Your voice Deep South under duress,
stress-dialect. "They already do,"
I say. "Name, address, taxpayer ID #.

Right here on these labels." But you're back
inside a bamboo blind, trail of smoke
between paddy fields. Memories

we've told each other that itemize
our fears: delayed reactions'
anodyne that almost could have healed us.

Your third-degree dreams gagged
and bound to a broken stool,
the interrogator's pistol pressed against

your temple, her voice in your ear
a bullet slipping in its chamber.
You stand with the others against

barbed wire, between curfew sirens
and blood money whispering
Shoot to *Kill.* You go on wrestling

your shadows. What might change
the bottom line between lovers? Who else
would finish your taxes for you?

II. Blues for Imhotep

. . . Unloved in the
Crescent City, I sat in a bathtub

clutching a straight razor.

Your forehead is scored with wishful
      thinking's hieroglyphs. Where am I
           that April day you sit in the bathtub

of our shotgun house in the Bywater
      pressing a straight razor to your night-
           wise skin because I don't love you?

Pre-emptive lacerations. Pharaoh's scythe
      and flail you've crossed over your breast
           to deflect Osiris's viridian eye. Yes,

I remember that pearl-handled blade
      on its glass shelf behind the bathroom mirror
           next to the brass hook for towels where

I'd come upon the other woman's night-dress,
      that winding sheet of our marriage.
           So don't talk to me about sealed mouths

planting kisses on desire's breath-map.
      I've made it a life's work to love you,
           who wears silence like an amulet, a *kaa*

to precede your stone boat to the underworld
      where funerary cartouches would fill with your self-
           willed name, its Ptolemaic syllables.

Why do you think I sat you down
          on a packing box's sarcophagus lid
                    and said, *"This can't go on."*?

I am not gone. In the Crescent City's
          dense, Nilotic air, how far
                    back to bloodstone do we have

to question? *Do what you gotta do,*
          you tell me, and get up to bathe. I
                    linger in the room,

balancing in a lapis lazuli trance
          on your stepladder. I run my hands
                    over antique molding you've scraped

and sanded almost to innocence. I know
          a word broken from Ma'at's hieratic
                    friezes even now could save us.

Regret I will roll up the sandstone ramp
          of years like a Sisyphus beetle's dungball,
                    under the pitiless gaze of Amun-Ra.

Then I hear your laugh from the bathroom
          in the back of the house, and move
                    down the dusty hallway toward you.

III. Syllabics: Dancing to Death

Who was that girl who danced to her death
in Mexico? That's what her memoir's
jacket paragraphs claimed: the second-

hand hardcover you handed to me
—*See what I'm reading?*—as I boxed up
my books to leave you. What did we want

from her? Darlene: was that her name?
Her panicked face glancing backward from
the author photo: silver clips in

her blonde frizz didn't hide her gaping
ear hole, blue cloud of smoke from the hand-
rolled cigarette she pinched between nail-

bitten fingers, stinging both our eyes.
In breaks between taping up boxes
I skimmed her first chapters, then couldn't

put her down—the book turned a woman
I hoped never to become: slamming
herself against peeling plaster walls

of some *cantina* in Jalisco,
reeling with tequila and fever
that had eaten into her inner

ear since her first boyfriend had beaten
her, left her for dead at the border.
El oído carcomido in

the mortally mellifluous tongue
of her Oaxacan gigolo, who
pimped her on the plaza to pay for

smack, speed, and her working girl's boudoir
above the bar. Why did you want me
to read her? I was losing my own

balance, skimming her chapters faster
and faster, dancing frantic tangos
with her across the pages, losing

my own way in that no-kind-of-life
she wanted to flee, and I wanted
to flee with her. I slipped her into

my last carton, hoping you wouldn't
miss her. Next day you stood over me
glowering: *Where is she?* Which of us

were you demanding? I couldn't lie
very long, I slit open my last
packed box, and pulled her out from her nest

beneath files: years of your love letters.
I never read her final chapters,
another life I couldn't borrow.

I handed her over—your big hands
took her in. Where is she now? The last
woman about whom we would argue.

IV. Round: What Love Is

I am never Aphrodite's fool
these afternoons in spring's deep
song, all our belongings stacked
in this shotgun house's makeshift rooms
while an old standard turns

on the dusty turntable: *You Don't Know
What Love Is.* At my battered desk
I cross out words, and you at your butcher-
block table in the back room
tap and scat a blank page

into deepening song. But where
are my most recent pages? I glance around
the half-assembled middle room—shelves
stacked with paperbacks, rocking chair
with broken rungs, mousetrap under

the Sears Roebuck blue divan: empty
as a mixed blessing on this house.
"Where are my last pages?" I ask aloud.
Don't look at me, you snap, scattering
my glance across the half-assembled shelves

and the turntable whose saxophone blows
that old tune back into the Crescent City's
deepening afternoon. Where indeed, my scattered
leaves, until my glance deflects into
undissembled trash and the tisket-

a-tasket we joked in happier days
was Ella's yellow basket: scrap pages balled
and tossed in afternoon's full-spectrum light
pouring over the transom. My pages.
I pluck them from the wastebasket

and uncrumple their yellowing matte—
no match for an old torch song's questioning
or Piety Street's unwritten lines. No inkling
of the line I cross when I step into
our shotgun back room and shake

my rescued pages in your face. What
is my unscripted accusation? Who else
has walked through these disheveled rooms,
rummaged these unlevel shelves? You
glance away: "*I don't know nothing.*"

The unknown saxophone rises
to a crescendo, and I step into the space
between your table and your chair,
your voice in my ear like a fast script's
insistent lines, *I don't know nothing*

and my voice empty of dissembling—
no smoky-throated singer but what you've called
lopsided girl, I watch my hand take a page
from your table and tear it cleanly
down the middle: "*Now you know*

how it feels." Then I lay each torn half
down where I found it   and your big hand raises
lands dead-on my temple, shatters
my glasses   my face in slow-motion   In
the concussion of incongruous music

blurring there   I am someone else
who witnesses   lenses and frames
scatter on the pitted floorboards, which one
of us is shouting   whose breath crumples
and uncrumples   what unlevel playing field

this floor we cross   these shotgun rooms'
roar in my pulse   my hands blur
over the phone but my fingers know
who to call   my fingers find the numbers
. . . *nine* . . . like a dancer's turn . . . *one* . . .

a cool, cerulean tune   you step-turn
away, my fingers do the walking
. . . *one* . . . on the sleepless key pad. "*No!*"
you shout from the empty front room.
"*Don't call them!*" Who decides

that I hang up, as fear's echoes
crumple against the empty walls? Too
late: two cops blurt through the blurred front
door and grab you: slight, gray-faced,
shaking like passion's spectral hostage.

A scene burned in freeze-frame through
memory's unfiled charges. Do I know then
what connects, divides our differing skins? I never
recognize the broken-hearted singer, but
I am never Aphrodite's fool.

VI REFLECTIONS IN BLUE

What If?

The two white cops hadn't erupted into
our front room, empty of everything
but stepladder, carpenter's level, and the echo
of a blow? If they hadn't vice-
gripped you by your lapidary
arms, your face gray as slate
and drained of everything but itself?

What if paint scrapers and sander parts
hadn't bulged from pockets of your coveralls,
wood shavings hadn't curled like blond
indictments in your uncombed hair,
the fruit of sweat and troubled
equity, love's undocumented loans?

If I hadn't stood there, hackles
high in shocked homage to the Beast
Within, and when the cops barked
Whadda we do with him
lady?, what if my anger didn't break
the trance, and I hadn't stumbled
upon my own slow diastolic

measure, a single melodic line
searching itself out in darkness
the way lovers once echo-located each
other? If I hadn't startled
myself back into the room?
If I'd answered, *Take*
him away.

What if they'd read you
your Miranda rights, then shackled
ankles and wrists shrunken in denim
cuffs, and hauled you in
like a flounder at the telltale end
of its camouflage? Run brain scans
in the squad car, and fingered
your wallet flat for jailbait
while I signed their bad actors'
prompt book with your real name?

What if the metal detectors
had flashed red as they hustled
you past lockdown, and Storyville
had morphed to Angola's anteroom
while I sweet-talked the mortgage lender
into buying back the house? Little
me: born out of reach of the 'Nam
and its National Draft, my brothers

burning their high-stakes numbers.
Little me—those shotgun rooms
in the Crescent City's mephitic spring
my only Combat Zone
and Finisterre. Little me,
mistress of no debility
but my own. *You're on your own,
kid,* said the paternal echoes in my head
when I stepped across the color line.

Could I have taken matters into
someone else's hands? Crawled back
from the slammer where
I'd absented you, to pick up
my glasses slapped across the floor

or *cry me a river* in full view
of the guard towers?

       What if I'd settled
your affairs, sealed my own fate
with hell's power of attorney? If
I'd finally sprung you
and we'd faced each other
across the bedroom's bruise-blue
swelter, if I'd held out my hands
with their broken nails, my lucky numbers
extinguished in your eyes?

       Then what of your scot-
free metamorphoses, bright
moments in the third-degree
klieg lights? Thanks to me
your rap sheet in the sweet thereafter
shorter than a bebop *koan,*
all charges against you
zeroed out.

What if? That prestidigitator's
second grasp, the year 2000's non-compliant
heart running its computer simulations.
Where we would be now. Futility's
pushups, absences we talk to
in the mirrors? Or adversaries
in each other's arms, both of us
collecting life sentences like paychecks
on the run?

I Forgive

my left hand for not hitting back
when Roy Otis's big hand slapped
the glasses off my face.

And I forgive my left arm for not rising to block
his open palm coming toward me.

I forgive my right hand for dialing 9-1-1,
for hanging up when he yelled "*No*"
and I heard the wanted man's terror in his voice.

I forgive my ears for hearing the patrol car
roll up a minute later and screech to a stop.

I forgive my eyes for watching two
beefy cops burst through the grille-work
door and straddle the front room's floorboards,

Roy Otis gray-faced with fear between them.
I forgive my heart for being glad.

When the white cop shifted his grip
and demanded, *Whadda we do with him,
Lady*? I forgive my tongue for saying

"Let him go."

Dixie White House Photo

No, I'm not ashamed to repeat myself.
I still desire that lean body
naked inside faded Levis
and checked shirt from Sears, biceps'
subtle bulge and the deltoids' ripple.
You lounge against the Dixie
White House wall, its *Members Only*
anguish in your face—too dark
beneath the Crescent City's mayhem
and honey creeper sky, cheekbones
too high to beg retelling,
West African maxillary contours.

I'm not ashamed to reiterate
the casual forward thrust of pelvis
under stiffened denim. Heft
and penetration, flutter-cries
of my breath and girl-come,
my lips that take you in.
No shame in the turmoil
of those hips, circlings of your tongue
on my nipples. Politics of my body
represented by yours.

                               The brick face
stripped, its exclusionary slogan
losing its grip—paint striated, resisting jet
reflections in your eyes. I apologize
for what you see—my eyes through the lens
already glancing away as I snap
the shutter. I'm not ashamed, I've kept
that black and white exposure.

What You Gave Me

(Seventeen American Sentences)

A book with scattered skulls and tipped tombstones on a glossy red cover.

A dedication scrawled on the title page: *To You, My Other Self.*

A kitchen witch on a broomstick flying on a string above the sink.

Where did she zoom off, from the first apartment I lived in after you?

Mouse puppet that peered from your hand around the door—
bright-eyed and fuzzy.

I propped it upright on the telephoto lens of my Minolta.

A turquoise amulet with broken clasp, on a strand of black trade beads.

A hippie jeweler fixed it on his tarp on Telegraph Avenue.

More books—Borges, Villón, Césaire, Langston Hughes, Wakoski, Kafka.

Letters twice a week, that Fall you lived with your grandmother, out of work.

Letters in your slanted cursive, on blue-lined scholar's stationery.

A tape of "Billy Jean" from when Michael Jackson's face was still his own.

Two summer skirts, an Indian blouse, but not the blue-flowered sofa.

What I lent you for the shotgun house? What you've paid back? Almost zero.

A freeloader tenant's phone bill you forwarded months later, to my mom.

Incensed, she called you: *My daughter left that phone in her name
to help you.*

You pay this bill. It's your problem, not my daughter's. You replied,
Yes, Ma'am.

Crossing a Line: a Round

I'm the only one to buy her book—
that young woman who sits by herself
at the same signing table as you,

whose signing line snakes around the room
and out the door. The younger poet
who's read first—your opening act—whose first

small book sits in a tidy pile beside her
at the signing table, beside you who signs
book after book, and for some admirers

multiple copies. She sits by herself
in a black silk frock, silk stole with
iridescent shimmer, blush pearls—an opening

actor's giveaway? Her unsold books
welling up in her eyes. I stand
by myself by the signing table.

I already own your books, a row
of spines I've stood on their own lengthening
shelf—you gifted me the first ones,

didn't you? Their dedications across years
of title pages are wishful thoughts
we can no longer admit to

or deny. I step across the space
between your line and hers, that opening
shimmer between a first thought

and a wishful signature's giveaway.
I make myself a line of one in front of her
and buy her book. How far

out of line have I stepped?
Eyes bright, she signs her title page,
makes change, and hands me

my copy, her face level and unchanged. *Oh,*
you glance over: *I should do that,*
too. You stand up from your place

at the signing table and step around
behind her, while the line
wishing itself forward toward you

stops in a domino ripple. You stand
beside her, pick up her book, and her face
outdoes itself—her eyes embrace you

in a grateful cascade of dedications.
The line waiting for you to sign
watches as you embrace her,

your hands opening her chances
like a string of pearls. Where am I
outside this line-up? You take

your place again and go on signing.
Your buyers fall into this second line
like dominoes, and buy her book,

too—filling her hands with proofs
of purchase. Her signature ripples
across pages of self-made narratives,

her opening act outdoes itself
in a cascade of chances, and I stand by
with our history of wishful giveaways.

What have I changed by going
first, crossing a line—at first
the only one to buy her book?

Ghazal: Other Than Yours

—beginning with a line by Faiz Ahmed Faiz

How could one weep for sorrows other than yours?
That grief-struck summer I seek no refuge other than yours.

In that midnight room, alone with you after so long,
I want no deep song other than yours.

Night descends its spiral staircase, unfolds its sable
patterns on the bed, no skin satin other than yours.

You're my Shiva with a blues guitar
I teased you once. What laughter in those days other than yours?

Will you get in trouble for this? Your question as you take me.
Whose trouble? Whose face on the pillow other than yours?

Those ghosts, our years together. Have I crossed
three states for embraces other than yours?

Forget those foolish nights. In tears I quote myself.
No past lies down with the present other than yours.

Your skin's scent of musk and arrowroot, could I
forget? No flesh rises between my hands other than yours.

Shiva's marble-veined haft I ride all night.
Whose body speaks through dreams other than yours?

All night between my lips, questions I mean
to ask. All night, no sweet oblivion other than yours.

If you say the word, I'll stay. You slide to the bed's
far end—what silence so eloquent other than yours?

For weeks I would cry out to you in dreams.
No steps would retrace themselves in dreams other than yours.

We have it out in dreams, in dreams as we
never had. What debts recollected other than yours?

Next morning, you're miles away across the room.
No history won from struggles other than yours.

Faiz cried, *Don't ask me for that love again!* That morning
I drive away alone, over a horizon other than yours.

(Translation of lines from Faiz Ahmed Faiz by Agha Shahid Ali.)

Sestina: *"That mouth . . ."*

"*. . . always going,*" you taunt, as I gab on the phone
with poets from Napoleon's Bar: your nervous lover
blowing plosives and palatals into the rum-colored
mouthpiece. My face flushed as the season's
Zephyr-cheeks, puffing from the celestial edges
of old maps, trying to scare up a storm.

Our shotgun house lists on its storm-
pilings. "*Girl, you carrying on that phone
like there's no tomorrow.*" That Beulah Baptist edge
to your voice, the plea I miss: blame's lover
fixing the house from the inside, season
of sweat and fragile equity you strip old color

from the sheetrock. Our balance sheet is colored
red, like tempest clouds that agitate a firestorm
survivor. Unsecured debt and the hurricane season
come around again. *Get off that phone
and talk to <u>me</u>,* you mean. *Who else is your lover?*
Your unvoiced question with its double edge.

We're tired of living on the edge,
taking our losses up-front. Would the sky's color
change its mind? Could we go on as lovers
as our self-protective gestures—those private storms—
sink into the vortex of the telephone's
receiver, reverse polarities of the season?

We already lean into another season.
You embrace your own shadow at the room's far edge.
"Take me as I am," I say, and hang up the phone.
Weapons in your concealed history scare me, color
of your skin a risk we share, desire like a summer storm
I almost could have married, if I were a lover

who could smile past your other lovers.
Could I smile now, years too late to give our season
another chance? My leaving you: a freak storm
that gathered its own momentum. Reasons I acknowledge,
debts to each other deferred: memory's colors
don't fade from your voice, on today's blue telephone.

The season bleeds into another decade's color,
millennial storms are on the rise. You're on edge
now, on the phone with me. But who else is your lover?

Pantoum: Letter to a Known Stranger

How much longer could she trust his hands,
in love with her heretic prayers—
hands stroking her awake at dawn,
the unprotected edge of speech?

Did love of her heretic prayers
waver on his oscillograph of shadows
at the unprotected edge of speech?
Again and again their half-occluded sleep

wavered, and an oscillation of shadows
played hide-and-seek between the fortune teller's laughs.
Again and again in half-occluded sleep
they were happy and unhappy in the same breath,

playing hide-and-seek between the fortune teller's laughs
in a *tableau vivant* of wishful psalms.
They were happy and unhappy in the same breath,
their reflections gestures for what they could not name

in a *tableau vivant* of wishful psalms.
Would they kiss on facing pages of a book,
their reflections gestures for what they could not name—
memories that hurt them into song?

Now they kiss on facing pages of a book,
their years wind backward in the mirrors
and memories hurt them into song.
Their stumble-dance into the dark

rewinds their years like film within the mirrors.
Could she have guessed she'd fool herself
in that stumble-dance into the dark?
How else to talk with the dead without clairvoyance?

Let her confess: she fooled herself
as he stroked her awake at dawn.
How else to talk with the dead without clairvoyance?
How much longer could she trust his hands?

Shadow Palimpsests

after Bob Perelman, "Chronic Meanings"

Unfinished business, we could have
remorse or suicide, not yet
scrolling our lost coordinates into
friends gone AWOL in some
powers smaller than our notice

you knew the score, but
no dress reddening with every
friend's child who came upon
the studio's single shaded bulb
like back-dated options, where

your steps retraced themselves and
the crime scene taped off
one helluva down payment on
symptom or contagion, who knows
we weren't trying to change

that child a decoy for
did I forgive your hand
everything tied to *Baby, please*
who died a thousand times
sitting you down to say

we've erased the years between
the child found dead under
a blur in closet mirrors
you in fading coveralls, then
entered into that code-switch

accents crawling backward on hands
no statute of limitations on
our desires played hide and
secrets long deferred like dresses
like a necromancer's aura, you

sifting gumbo *filé* and paprika
our love always mortgaged to
Talk to me, Baby, please
every man's lucky charm, before
the lights within our bodies

how else to speak with
your slant, meticulous hand, not
that other woman's dress under
a foxhole you almost didn't
life savings and their crawl

that child struggled hard but
close calls canceled out our
stumble across the color line
other women's eyes, unbending signatures
no decoys for any future

dead without clairvoyance, old dreams
Gotta keep movin' on, until
heart's lanes color of regret
did we fool ourselves with
stumble-dance into the dark

hook behind our bathroom door
Napoleonic ne'er-do-wells strolled

blood cash that spilled from
dreams and their costly evasions
that woman's dress, *Not red*

not coffins yet, lined up
your child fighting for his
two-timed, blue-lined letters
hurtling down some headlong road
what else could I tell

The Devil and the Angel

Devil:

I know. I know
you blame me, don't you?
You're thinking, "Why is he
up here on Machu Picchu
anyway?" But I belong wherever you are.

Angel:

Blame? No, no. No more.
Not after August's meteor showers
have hailed down on these ancient
fitted stones. After sun spots
have risen above their eleven-year
vortices of storm, reversed
their dark polarities. Blame?
Not after the quantum arcs of angels,
winged photons' glow around
the nerve-ends. No demon, love.
Earth's logic doing its dumb
dim best, trying to catch up
to the intelligence that turns
the spheres.
                My white dress lifts
in this solar wind. The body takes itself
for its own shadowprint. You belong
where no time has passed
in these leaps across the synapses.

Lucifer—glimmer inside a thought,
epiphany and pridefall. Not
in opposition. Radiant darkness
defused by light. I am the Angel

of No Losses, one wing in debt
divided, connected by the sun's
infernal touchstone. Welcome
to my world. The demons are intrigued
by our hard choices.

Acknowledgments

Grateful acknowledgment is made to the periodicals and anthologies in which many of these poems first appeared:

Bacopa Literary Review: "Sestina: '*That mouth . . .*'"
Brilliant Corners: "Faubourg-Marigny"
Glassworks: "Aubade: Still Life"
Harbor Review: "Ghazal: Other Than Yours"
The MacGuffin: "'Hello, World'"
The Missouri Review: "Heat Wave: Liberty, Missouri"
New Letters: "Note From the Stop-Gap Motor Inn"
Nimrod: "Another Country," "The Divide: New Orleans"
Ninth Letter: "Credo in Blue: New Orleans"
North American Review: "Blue Mitosis"
One Magazine: "Epithalamion in Blue"
Pandemic Publications: "Endecasyllabics: About the Women (Ruthie),"
    "Endecasyllabics: About the Women (Meredith, Melody)"
Ploughshares: "Masquerade"
Post Road: "Betty Carter at the Blue Room," "Dixie White House Photo"
Presence: A Journal of Catholic Poetry: "I Forgive"
Rattle: "Triolets on a Dune Shack"
Raven Chronicles: "The Putting-Off Dance"
Rise Up Review: "Another Country"
Seattle Review: "Faubourg-Marigny"
The Southern Review: "One Afternoon on Royal Street"
Tahoma Literary Review: "Fire Season"
Triquarterly: "Through Bus Windows: Seattle"
Witness: "Shadow Palimpsests"
Women's Review of Books: "White," "Of Omission"

"Masquerade," "Note From the Stop-Gap Motor Inn," and "Heat Wave: Liberty, Missouri" were reprinted in earlier forms in the chapbook *From a White Woman's Journal* (Water Mark Press, 1985; second printing, 1994).

"Note From the Stop-Gap Motor Inn" was included in *Cape Discovery: The Fine Arts Work Center Anthology,* edited by Bruce Smith and Catherine Gammon (Sheep Meadow Press, 1994); and in *Poets of the New Century*, edited by Richard Higgerson and Roger Weingarten (David R. Godine, 2001).

"Heat Wave: Liberty, Missouri" was included in *American Diaspora: Poetry of Displacement*, edited by Virgil Suárez and Ryan G. Van Cleave (University of Iowa Press, 2001). Copyright © 2002 by Carolyne Wright.

"Heat Wave: Liberty, Missouri" was reprinted in the chapbook *Greatest Hits 1975 - 2001* (Pudding House Publications, 2002).

"Another Country" and "The Divide: New Orleans" were finalists for the Hardman/Pablo Neruda Prize for Poetry (*Nimrod,* 2001).

"Blue Mitosis" was a finalist for the James Hearst Prize in Poetry (*North American Review*, 2003).

"On Learning That I'm Not C. D. Wright, Couple Walks Out of Maple Leaf Bar" was published in *Umpteen Ways of Looking at a Possum: Critical and Creative Responses to Everette Maddox,* edited by Grace Bauer and Julie Kane (Xavier Review Press, 2006).

"Blue Mitosis" was reprinted in *Harbor Review: Special Issue: Abortion* (May 2019).

"I Forgive" appeared on *Verse Daily* on April 6, 2021; and was reprinted in *When Home Is Not Safe: Writing on Domestic Verbal, Emotional, and Physical Abuse,* edited by Linera Lucas and Judith Skillman (McFarland/Exposit Books, 2021).

"Shadow Palimpsests" was nominated for a 2019 Best of the Net Awards in 2020.

"Triolets on a Dune Shack" appeared on *Verse Daily,* versedaily.com, May 25, 2020; in *The Poetry Newsletter,* June 2020; and in *The Strategic Poet,* edited by Diane Lockward. (Terrapin Books, 2021).

I am grateful to 4Culture (the King County Arts Commission), the Brush Creek Foundation, the Dorland Mountain Colony, the Fine Arts Work Center in Provincetown, the Instituto Sacatar, Jentel / The Pushcart Foundation, the National Endowment for the Arts, the National Endowment for the Humanities, the Seattle Office of Arts & Culture (formerly the Seattle Arts Commission), the Santa Fe Art Institute, the Summer Literary Seminar (St. Petersburg), the Vermont College Post-Graduate Writers' Conference, the Vermont Studio Center, and the Witter Bynner Foundation for Poetry for support and encouragement while I was working on this book.

Thanks also to the following colleges, universities, writing programs and literary centers where I served as visiting poet, professor of creative writing, or in other faculty roles when the events in these poems occurred, and later when I was writing and revising these poems:

St. Lawrence University, William Jewell College, University of Wyoming, Emory University, University of Miami, Oklahoma State University, University of Central Oklahoma, University of Oklahoma, The College of Wooster, Cleveland State University, Whidbey Writers Workshop / Northwest Institute of Literary Arts MFA Program, Richard Hugo House, Lynchburg College, Seattle University, University of Washington - Bothell, Antioch University MFA Program.

Thanks to friends and fellow poets and writers who listened; who read and commented, in manuscript conferences and consultations as well as in conversation;

and who gave helpful suggestions about these poems while they were in progress. I am grateful for their dedicated attention and support:

Christopher Bursk, Denise Duhamel, Margaret Henderson, Sarah Jones, Stephanie Painter, Ed Pavlić, David Rigsbee, Ed Skoog, Elaine Smokewood, Mary Ellen Talley, Charles Harper Webb, Roger Weingarten, Deborah Woodard; and the members of the Greenwood Poets Group and the Folio Poetry Society.

Gratitude as well to editors and guest editors of literary magazines and anthologies not already named above who have supported this work:

Mary Bast, Robin Becker, Allison Blevins, Phoebe Bosché, Jennifer Bosveld, Christopher Boucher, Kelly Davio, Jessica Faust, Sascha Feinstein, Coco Gordon, Vince Gotera, Tim Green, Christopher Howell, Gary Copeland Lilley, Kaye Linden, Kathleen McClung, Mary Ann B. Miller, Speer Morgan, David Ray, Francine Ringold, Lois Roma-Deeley, Gregory Stapp, and Jeri Theriault. Greatest of thanks as ever to Christine Holbert—Founding Editor, Publisher, and Book Designer Extraordinaire of Lost Horse Press—for her belief in my work, and her friendship. And infinite gratitude to my husband and undercover poet, Jim Parrott, for his insights, inspiration, and love.